An
Overview
for
Teens

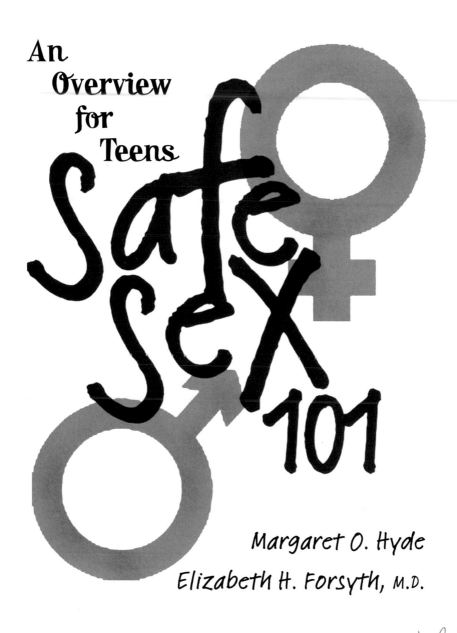

# Safe Sex 101

Margaret O. Hyde

Elizabeth H. Forsyth, M.D.

Twenty-First Century Books • Minneapolis

Twenty-First Century Books
A division of Lerner Publishing Group
241 First Avenue North
Minneapolis, Minnesota 55401 U.S.A.
Website address: www.lernerbooks.com

Illustrations courtesy of Sharon Lane Holm

Photographs are reproduced with permission from: © Michael Newman/Photo Edit: pp. 17, 86; © Jonathan Nourok/Photo Edit: p. 21; AP/Wide World Photos: pp. 23, 42, 96; © Reuters/CORBIS: p. 26; © Paolo Pellegrin/Magnum Photos: p. 32; © Malcolm Linton/Liaison/Getty Images: p. 34; © Bill Freeman/Photo Edit: p. 44; © Gideon Mendel/CORBIS: p. 48; © Mary Kate Denny/Photo Edit: p. 63; © David M. Phillips/Photo Researchers, Inc.: p. 73; © M. Long/Visuals Unlimited: p. 82; © Ray Ellis/Photo Researchers, Inc.: p. 85; © SIU/Visuals Unlimited: p. 87; © Scott Camazine & Sue Trainor/Photo Researchers, Inc.: p. 89; © BURGER/Photo Researchers, Inc: p. 90; © Gusto/Photo Researchers, Inc.: p. 91; © Saturn Stills/Photo Researchers, Inc.: p. 92; © David Butow/CORBIS SABA: p. 106.

Library of Congress Cataloging-in-Publication Data

Hyde, Margaret O. (Margaret Oldroyd)
    Safe sex 101 : an overview for teens / by Margaret O. Hyde and
  Elizabeth H. Forsyth.
      p.   cm. — (Teen overviews)
    Includes bibliographical references and index.
    ISBN-13: 978-0-8225-3439-6 (lib. bdg. : alk. paper)
    ISBN-10: 0-8225-3439-8 (lib. bdg. : alk. paper)
    1. Teenagers—Sexual behavior.   2. Safe sex in AIDS prevention.
  3. Birth control.   4. Sexually transmitted diseases.   I. Title.   II. Series.
  HQ35.H93 2006                   613.9'071—dc22                 2005018806

Manufactured in the United States of America
1 2 3 4 5 6 – BP – 11 10 09 08 07 06

# Contents

## Chapter 1
How Do You Decide If
You Are Ready for Sex?                                    5

## Chapter 2
Do You Choose Abstinence?                                 19

## Chapter 3
Why Learn about Safe Sex?                                 37

## Chapter 4
Secret Lives of Teens 54

## Chapter 5
Where You Can Learn about Safe Sex 61

## Chapter 6
How Your Sex Organs Work 71

## Chapter 7
What You Should Know about Contraception 80

## Chapter 8
Working to Prevent Teen Pregnancy and
Sexually Transmitted Diseases 101

Glossary 109

For Further Information 115

Source Notes 119

Index 125

## Chapter 1

# How Do You Decide If You Are Ready for Sex?

You are sure you are in love with a person you have known for a long time. You have intense feelings that are much more than a physical attraction. Your love is part of a caring relationship based on mutual trust and friendship, and you feel wonderful when you are with the person you love. He or she makes you feel special. You know you should wait longer before having sex, but you are finding it more and more difficult to wait. You both want to make a decision about having sex. You know that there is no 100 percent safe sex, but knowing about contraception and sexually transmitted diseases is only part of the picture. How do you know if you are ready?

# Ethan and Kate: The Pressure to Have Sex

Ethan had been thinking all day about having sex. In fact, he thought about it every day. But today he would have a chance to be alone with Kate. Her parents would be away for at least three hours after school. He was looking forward to losing his virginity with the girl he loved. Kate and Ethan, now sixteen, had been together for two years, and they had been very close sexually. Ethan was sure they would make it all the way today.

Kate was excited, too. A few hours alone with Ethan were very special, but she had decided just how far she would go. She was not ready for sexual intercourse. She knew Ethan was going to pressure her to go all the way. To her, this was the ultimate act of love, and she wanted to wait. She knew she loved Ethan. She couldn't imagine life without him, but she was not ready for the kind of sex he wanted and she knew it. Kate wanted to wait until they finished school and until they were married.

When Ethan arrived at Kate's house that afternoon, he saw her mother's car in the driveway. What had gone wrong? Was Kate sick? Her mother greeted Ethan warmly, and Kate tried to sound casual when she told him about the change in plans. Kate had talked to her mother about how to say no to Ethan if he pressured her for sex, and her mother thought staying home for the afternoon would make things easier for Kate. Kate had wanted to be alone with Ethan and she was prepared to say, "No, I am not ready to have sex," if he pressured her. She had already told him she really loved him, but she meant it when she said she was not ready. Since Kate's mother was home, Ethan and Kate went to a private place near the hockey field to discuss sex. Ethan loved Kate, and he was willing to wait because that is what she wanted.

Many teens who have given in to the pressure to have sex say, "I didn't know how to say no"; "I didn't want to hurt his/her feelings"; or "I didn't want to lose him/her." If your partner doesn't stay with you after you refuse to have intercourse, he/she may not really have strong feelings for you. Also, many people make bad decisions about sex after using alcohol or other drugs. Being drunk or stoned impairs your ability to make a wise choice.

## Help in Saying "No"

How can you say "no" when you are not ready for sex? Make a list of the reasons you want to wait and have a plan about how you will deal with someone who pressures you to have sex. Are you prepared to leave the situation by just walking away?

Be ready for the following questions (they apply to both sexes) and think about possible replies:

1. "Don't you love me? You know I love you."
   *Reply:* "Of course I love you, but I wouldn't respect myself if I broke my vow to wait until we are married."

2. "Intercourse will bring us closer together."
   *Reply:* "If we have to worry about pregnancy, it will take us farther apart."

3. "Everyone's doing it. Why won't you?"
   Reply: "About half the kids in high school aren't. Even if they were, that doesn't mean I have to. "

4. "Show me you really love me."
   *Reply:* "I'm showing you how much I love you by waiting."

5. "Nothing bad will happen to you. Are you afraid to love me completely?"
   *Reply:* "I'm sure you don't have AIDS, but something will happen to me emotionally. I'm not ready for that."

6. "We've been in love for years, why don't you trust me?"
   *Reply:* "I just don't feel comfortable about the risk right now. "

7. "Don't you like boys (girls)?"
   *Reply:* "I like them, but I don't want to become so involved with any right now."

8. "Abstinence is no fun."
   *Reply:* "Neither is having a baby when you are not ready for it. I don't want an STD, either."

9. "I have a condom."
   *Reply:* "A condom won't protect me from emotional hurt."

10. "I'll always love you. We need to share this experience."
    *Reply:* "If you'll always love me, you can wait until I am ready."

11. "Won't you change your mind?"
    *Reply:* "I'll say no again and again until you
    realize I mean it."

You can practice saying no before the occasion
arises. When it does, speak confidently and look the
person straight in the eye. If the situation seems to be
getting difficult, you can leave.

## At a Party

Suppose you are a girl who meets a terrific boy at a
party and you are excited because he shows an
interest in you. You talk for a while and are flattered
by all the attention he gives you. He puts his arm
around you, and you find yourself going into a room
far from the rest of the party. You really like him, but
you are not ready for what he has in mind. You love
the feeling of being close to him, but you know you
have to put on the brakes, even if it kills your chances
of having a relationship with him. You try to stay cool.

You take a deep breath, smile, and tell him to put
the condom away. You aren't interested in having a
physical relationship with him at this point. He tries
to change your mind with promises and flattery, but
you know if he really cares about you, he will respect
your feelings and not push you into something you
are not ready to do.

Your heart sinks. He leaves, and you know he just
wanted you for sex. But do you really want him if that
is all he cares about? You can find someone later who
wants to have a real relationship with you, and he can
find someone who is willing to just have sex.

How do you react if you are a boy who is pressured by a girl? Are you willing to become involved with a girl if you don't really care for her? Can you tell her to back off without hurting her feelings?

## Hooking Up

Fifteen-year-old Mia wondered if she was ready for what she was told "everybody" was doing. Some of the girls she hung out with had promised to stay virgins until they were married. Now they were hooking up, having oral sex, as a way they believed let them stay virgins and still have sex without getting pregnant. A hookup is an encounter that may involve anything from kissing to sexual intercourse, but it usually means oral sex. Hooking up is usually a quick sexual encounter, but it can bring intense feelings and emotional problems afterward.

Mia's friends told her she should try oral sex. Her friends met boys at the mall, who were casual friends and sometimes strangers, and had oral sex with them in out-of-the-way places. The girls used their tongues and mouths on the boys' penises until the boys ejaculated, or released their semen. Often the hookup was a onetime thing; the girls never met with the boys again. If a relationship developed from hooking up, that was OK, but it was not expected. Nobody had to worry about getting pregnant and there was no responsibility involved. Most of the girls had no idea that they were risking AIDS and other sexually transmitted diseases. Some girls worried because a hookup left them feeling confused and disillusioned. Feelings of anxiety, sadness, worry, and doubt were common.

Mia didn't want to become involved in hooking up, or with any kind of serious sex. She had hugged and kissed a few boys, but she wasn't ready to go any farther. Around the beginning of the spring semester, she had written to an advice columnist in her local newspaper asking if it was true that everyone was hooking up. She read the column day after day to see if her letter would be answered. On the day before spring vacation, there it was.

Dear Mia:

Hooking up can mean many different things. It can be anything from kissing to sexual intercourse, but it usually means a random sexual encounter in which a girl has oral sex with a boy. It is usually a situation where there is little social relationship. Some boys and girls hook up one time and never get together again for sex or any kind of socializing.

"Friends with benefits" is a term used to identify those who are willing to hook up without any serious relationship. A boy or girl might call one of these friends and decide on a meeting place where oral sex can be performed. This might be his or her place when parents are out, a closet in a building where they won't be interrupted, an out-of-the-way fire escape, the woods, or any place that they can be alone for a short while.

Those who have "friends with benefits" may include only a very small percentage of teens.

About half of today's teens are waiting for a serious relationship before having sex of any kind. Hooking up can be risky both medically and emotionally for boys as well as girls, since sexually transmitted diseases can be spread this way and serious emotional problems can follow. Most girls still want an emotional commitment from their sexual encounters rather than instant gratification.

Some teens who talk as if they have oral sex are just trying to make others believe that they do. If you refuse to do what your friends pressure you to do, you will not be the only one who doesn't hook up. You will be one who doesn't regret what you have done.

—Your Teen Adviser

News correspondent Katie Couric spoke with teens about sex on an NBC television program on January 26, 2005. Teens between the ages of thirteen and sixteen from all parts of the United States were asked questions about sex. In this group, 88 percent said they had not had oral sex. In another survey, released in September 2005 and based on data from the 2002 National Survey of Family Growth, just over half of teens (aged fifteen to nineteen) have had oral sex. About one in four who have not had sexual intercourse report that they have had oral sex.

# Making the Decision

Becoming sexually involved with another person, whether having oral sex or sexual intercourse, is a big step in your life. It's something to think about on your own long before you have to make a decision with anyone, even the partner you love deeply. It is probably one of the most important decisions you'll ever make.

Sixty-seven percent of sexually experienced teens say they wish they had waited longer before having sexual intercourse. Some said they did not consider the many feelings and responsibilities that can go with it. Some felt guilty because their religion does not approve of sex before marriage. Many find they wish they had waited for marriage. Both girls and boys may become infected with sexually transmitted diseases. Girls may become pregnant. Hearts may be broken by infidelity (cheating on someone) or the breakup of a relationship that was thought to be secure. Serious cases of depression may follow. These are just some of the things that can happen as a result of having sex before you are ready.

Caitlin, for example, is fifteen and says she has been tempted to have sex several times, especially after she has had a few beers. She loves Max and she is sure he loves her, but she is not ready to take such a big step. Caitlin says, "I know I'll do it sometime, but it won't be soon. I would be a mess if I had a baby. I can't even take care of myself. Besides, a lot of people who had sex when they were fifteen say they wish they had waited."

Some fifteen-year-olds have broken the law in their states concerning age of consent without realizing it, or perhaps without caring. A significant number of states have laws restricting young people's sexual activities. Is there a law in your state that makes it illegal for people younger than sixteen to have sexual relations? Age of consent ranges from fourteen to eighteen in the United States. In more than half of the states, the age of consent is sixteen.

Only you can decide if you are ready for sex. It makes sense to think about whether you want to have intercourse before you are presented with the situation. Here are some questions that may help you make a reasonable decision:

- Are you thinking about having sex because you believe everyone else your age is "doing it?" Even if it feels this way, it is important to realize that this is not true. According to a report from the Abstinence Clearinghouse, 54 percent of high school students say they have not had intercourse. It is not weird to wait for marriage. An increasing number of teens are doing so.

- What do you think might happen as a result of having sex? Do you understand the possible consequences and are you comfortable with them? If you plan to go to college, can you afford the time and money it takes to care for or to support a baby? Eight in ten pregnancies are unintended, and 79 percent of these babies are born to unmarried teens. Most teens believe that they are not ready to be pregnant or to become parents.

- Are you comfortable talking with your partner about sex and contraception? Have you learned about the use, benefits, and side effects associated with all forms of contraception? Choose a time when you and your partner can have a thoughtful, uninterrupted discussion. If you do not feel *completely* comfortable having this type of talk, you are not ready for sex.

- Are you both ready to be responsible for preventing pregnancy? If you plan to use a latex condom, be sure one is close when you might need it. Don't count on your partner being prepared. Since condoms can break, it is best to use two forms of birth control at once. No form of contraception is 100 percent safe.

- Do you both know how AIDS and other sexually transmitted diseases (STDs) are spread? Are you aware that when you have sex with your partner without protection you are exposed to all the diseases that he or she has been exposed to in previous relationships? Not everyone who has a sexually transmitted disease or infection knows it or has symptoms. If you or your partner has had another sex partner, both of you should consider being tested for STDs.

- Do you value your independence? Independence is a sign of maturity. Going along with someone else's decision is not. Sex should be an expression of love, not something a person feels pressured to do. You never owe someone sex.

- Do you agree that having sex is too important for a spur-of-the-moment decision? Sex can be an important part of a relationship, but it's not the most important thing. You can have a close relationship without sex.

- Do you have any moral, cultural, or religious convictions that might make having sex before marriage the wrong decision for you? Will you feel guilty or ashamed if you disregard these convictions?

- Are you ready to say "no" as many times as it takes to get your point across?

## Learning about Contraception

Almost everyone agrees that delaying sexual activity in adolescence is far better than being sexually active, even with protection. Nearly seven in ten teens do not think it is okay for high school teens to have sexual intercourse. Most parents and teens think it is important for teens not to have sex before they are married, but they also think it is important for them to receive information about birth control and protection from sexually transmitted diseases. This information can prevent unintended pregnancies and abortions. Even some pro-life advocates (people who oppose the termination of a pregnancy) support teaching safe sex as a way to prevent abortions.

Some people think teaching about contraception leads teenagers to have sex. The World Health Organization (WHO) and the U.S. National Campaign to Prevent Teen Pregnancy have conducted the two most exhaustive reviews of studies in this field. Both concluded that sex education programs do not promote or lead to an increase in

*Doctors are great sources of information about birth control and the prevention of sexually transmitted diseases.*

sexual activity among young people.

In the United States, about 35 percent of girls become pregnant at least once by the age of twenty. Eight in ten of these pregnancies are unintended, and 79 percent are to unmarried teens. The number one reason given by these teens for not using protection is that they weren't planning to have sex and it "just happened."

## Abstinence as a Method of Contraception

An increasing number of young people are choosing to abstain from sex until they are married. More than half of high school students are not sexually active. In one recent study among boys, only 46 percent said that they were sexually active. The number for girls was 47 percent, according to the National Center for Health Statistics. (This was the first time since the government began the survey in 1973 that the percentage of girls was higher than boys.)

Consistent abstinence is the only absolute way to prevent unintended pregnancy and sexually transmitted diseases, including HIV (human immunodeficiency virus, or the virus that causes AIDS). The next chapter in this book gives some information about abstinence, and may help you to decide if it is a good choice for you.

# Chapter 2

# Do You Choose Abstinence?

Are you part of the new sexual revolution? If your method of contraception is abstinence, you may be. Some people claim that abstinence is the new sexual revolution because it is becoming so popular and is the safest form of contraception. Not everyone agrees. The decline in teen pregnancy is due to the increase in teen abstinence, but it is also due to the increased use of condoms. Some say more condom use is the new sexual revolution. Whether fewer teens having babies is a result of abstinence, the increased use of condoms, or both, sexual habits are changing.

The first sexual revolution began in the late 1960s and early 1970s, when people began talking more openly about sex, viewing sexual scenes on television and in movie theaters, and listening to songs with sexually explicit lyrics. Books that were once banned for their sexual content became available at bookstores throughout the country. Sex manuals were placed prominently on store shelves, and the circulation of sexually oriented magazines increased. Contraceptives were improved and more commonly used, giving women control of their own reproduction. Some women chose to have both a family and a career. Today, in spite of women's progress in making their own reproductive decisions, young people are having babies at a very early age. Thirty-five percent of young women become pregnant at least once before they reach the age of twenty.

## Today's Teens Mature Earlier

Today, teenagers are maturing faster than previous generations of teens due to better health care and nutrition. Girls menstruate at a younger age, and boys become sexually mature earlier. Sexual feelings that used to arise in the mid-teens now occur by the early teens. As a result, about half of boys and girls lose their virginity in high school.

Along with these changes, almost everyone sees much more sex in the media. Do you have an idea of the number of sexual scenes you see in a week on TV, DVD, in magazines, and movies? Listen to the many references to sex in the lyrics of songs. Look at magazine ads and billboards and the computer screen. Sex is more explicitly discussed in fiction for young adults than it was in the past. All this makes a

*Look around you. Sex is used to sell almost every-thing from toothpaste to automobiles to tanning lotion. Can you count how many times a day you see sexual situations in advertisements?*

difference in how fast teens develop sexually

You probably have matured faster than your parents and grandparents, but even though teens are physically ready for sex sooner, the typical age for marriage has risen. Years ago, sixteen-year-olds had finished their education. Few people, except those who became doctors and lawyers, went on to college and graduate school. There were jobs on the farms and in the factories for teens, so they could support themselves and their families. They were considered to be ready for marriage. Today, many young people pursue education through their teens and well into their twenties. Many couples don't marry until they are in their mid-twenties or older, and some don't marry at all.

Girls are still having babies in their teens, and some are marrying at this early age, while many others feel comfortable as single mothers. The social stigma that once applied to unwed mothers has lessened, but many of the difficulties have not. Many unwed mothers are no longer in touch with the fathers of their babies. Some mothers don't know the names of the fathers, and some don't care. Some of these girls may have wanted a baby, but most did not.

The overwhelming majority of adolescents do not want to become parents in their teens. However, about 900,000 teens become pregnant each year. The rate of pregnancies to teens is declining, but it is still high. The United States has the highest rate of teen pregnancy in Western industrialized society; it is twice as high as in Canada and more than five times higher than in France, where the use of contraception is more common.

What do you think about teens, married or unmarried, having babies? Experts say that abstinence from sexual activity outside of marriage is the standard for all school-age boys and girls, but this standard is not always realistic. Suppose you decide you are not ready to have a baby, but you plan to become sexually active. Will you wait to think about contraception until *after* you find yourself in a sexually charged situation? Many teens do.

## Abstinence as a New Sexual Revolution

Abstinence is one kind of contraception that is growing in popularity. If you choose this method and stay with it, you will not become a parent and you will not get a sexually transmitted disease, such as AIDS. Abstinence is the choice of many teens.

*These teens sign a banner with the message "Say Not Yet" at a music festival in Minnesota. They are a few of the growing number of teens who have chosen abstinence as their lifestyle.*

Today's teens are changing their attitudes about abstinence. In the past, many teens thought of abstinence as an old-fashioned concept, and virginity carried a stigma. Consider the case of eighteen-year-old Sophia, who had remained a virgin. She thought everyone her age was having sex. Her friends talked about their experiences and called virgins geeks. Sophia told her friends that she had slept with a boy a few years earlier. She lied so her friends wouldn't make fun of her. After her school introduced an abstinence-only program, she was proud of being a virgin, and she was sorry she pretended she wasn't.

Many boys make a big deal out of losing their virginity. Some don't care who the girl is; they care more about telling their friends they have "done it." But that attitude is changing, too. In 2003, a study showed that only 26 percent of today's teens say that it is embarrassing to admit they are virgins. You might even see signs that say, "VIRGIN is not a dirty word," one of the messages being spread by abstinence-only supporters.

An increasing number of teens are proud of being virgins and remaining sexually abstinent until marriage. Sophia's cousin, Isabelle, is one of them. Isabelle has signed an abstinence pledge. She meets regularly with members of her church youth group, who think virginity is cool. Like some of the girls in her group, she wears a yellow bracelet to tell the world she will hug a boy, but she won't go any further.

Most of her friends wear purple bracelets to indicate that they will kiss any boy who takes the purple bracelets from their arms. Some girls are proud to show they will not go beyond kissing. Although no one in Isabelle's group wears bracelets of other colors, they know that wearing a red bracelet means girls are willing to lap dance (sit on a boy's lap fully clothed and rub up against him). A blue bracelet means girls will perform oral sex. Black bracelets are for those who have had sexual intercourse. Nobody in Sophia's or Isabelle's group wears a black bracelet.

Many girls who know the meaning of the colors of bracelets think the whole idea is stupid. For most teens, sex is a private matter. Some teens who have taken a pledge to be sexually abstinent until marriage wear silver rings with small, silver packages on them to show they are chaste. Some wear rings with "Jesus" engraved on them. Others wear rings with Christian crosses to show they believe in abstinence. Wearers are proud of their chastity rings. They say the rings remind them of their pledges and help them to remain abstinent.

In the abstinence program called True Love Waits, many teens take vows at ring parties that they will not have sex until they are married. The rings remind members of the group of their pledge:

> Believing that true love waits, I make a commitment to God, myself, my family, my friends, my future mate, and my future children to a lifetime of purity including sexual abstinence from this day until the day I enter a biblical marriage relationship.

Since this program is known as a biblical solution to life and is based on Christian beliefs, it does not appeal to many teens who are not religious or Christian. But anyone looking for support in an abstinence program can join programs such as True Love Waits without being involved in the religious beliefs.

Many abstinence programs, such as Life's Walk, Teen Aid, Sex Respect, Facts and Feelings, Worth the Wait, and Operation Keepsake, have started across the country. There are thousands of abstinence-until-marriage programs in the United States. A program called Choosing the Best is used in more than two thousand school districts in the United States. Girls in these programs feel safe from unwanted pregnancies. Boys in the programs prefer to wait until marriage for moral reasons, or because the girls they love want to wait.

*Young people from the Pure Love Alliance march in the streets of Philadelphia to promote abstinence and fidelity as a way to prevent teen pregnancy and sexually transmitted diseases.*

# Why Abstinence?

Many girls who choose sexual abstinence do so because they fear pregnancy. Both girls and boys mention fear of sexually transmitted diseases, fear of getting caught, religious reasons, and/or disapproval of their parents as reasons for choosing abstinence. Most people, including young people, agree that teens are too young to become parents.

An increasing number of young people are receiving abstinence-only education. Federal funding became available to many schools as far back as 1981, and by 2005, high schools in every state but California were receiving funding for abstinence-only programs. California refused federal funding for abstinence education in favor of more comprehensive sex education. Later, some states joined California in rejecting federal abstinence-only money by refusing to supply the matching funds needed to obtain it.

In Washington, the state legislature cut off matching funds for abstinence-only education because of increased public pressure. A letter to the governor from the Governor's Council on HIV/AIDS stated that the abstinence-only programs "do not give students complete information that they need to make responsible choices about their sexual activity." It also stated that the abstinence-until-marriage programs were harmful to gay and lesbian youth, because most states do not recognize gay marriage and those living in nontraditional households. The letter also claimed that abstinence-until-marriage programs offer "only shame and fear" to sexually abused youth.

Almost all teens are aware that they are the first generation to grow up in a world that includes HIV/AIDS, but most think it will not happen to them. They can be sure it won't only if they refrain from all sex, including oral and anal.

## Does Abstinence Include Oral and Anal Sex?

Everyone agrees that not having sex until marriage is abstinence, but not everyone agrees about the definition of sex, so the definition of abstinence varies. While everyone is a sexual human being from birth to old age, the expression of sex varies widely. Some girls prefer having sex with other girls, and some boys prefer boys. Most people mean sexual intercourse between a male and female when they talk about "doing it," but there are some who do not include oral and anal sex in the definition of sex. They believe that these are ways of having sex without getting pregnant or losing their virginity, so they are not really sex.

In the NBC/*People* National Survey of Young Teens' Sexual Attitudes and Behaviors, conducted in 2004, 54 percent of those questioned considered a teen who had had oral sex a virgin. Whether or not oral sex can be counted as abstinence depends on your definition. No matter what the definition, oral and anal sex can expose people to sexually transmitted diseases.

## Does Abstinence Work?

Controversy about abstinence-only programs in schools is widespread. According to those who favor abstinence-only programs, teens who are strong pledgers postpone sexual activity and are less likely to become pregnant. Some critics of the abstinence programs say otherwise, claiming no credible scientific research has found abstinence-only programs effective in delaying the onset of sexual intercourse, or reducing its frequency. However, some research reported in the August 2004 *Journal of Adolescent Health* credits abstinence-only programs with helping to reduce the pregnancy rate for fifteen- to seventeen-year-olds by as much as 53 percent.

In December 2004, U.S. representative Henry Waxman published a report titled, *Abstinence-Only Curricula Contain False Information*. According to this report, "Over 80 percent of the abstinence-only curricula . . . contain false, misleading, or distorted information about reproductive health." The report points to studies that prove abstinence-only programs increase the likelihood that participants will engage in risky behaviors by providing false information, such as suggestions that condom use does not prevent the transmission of HIV/AIDS. The Abstinence-Only Clearinghouse claimed the report was wrong, but vowed to check accuracy in its programs. In June 2005, false or misleading information was still reported in some programs.

Evaluations of programs vary, and much depends on what is being measured. In a report from the American Heritage Foundation, adolescents who take virginity pledges have lower rates of out-of-wedlock births. Controversy over how much abstinence-only programs work and how long students who participate in these programs remain abstinent is still widespread.

The American Medical Association (AMA), following the Waxman report, continued its position of supporting only community-based sex education that has evidence of solid results. The AMA's report said there is evidence that abstinence-only programs do not work for all adolescents.

Everyone agrees that teaching abstinence is a good thing, but many experts say that it's not wise to make this the only message. Both teens and adults, including medical experts and public-health officials, overwhelmingly believe that young people should be given a strong abstinence message *and* straightforward, detailed information about contraception.

Abstinence is 100 percent safe if one does not break one's pledge, but those who break it are not prepared to have safe sex. Critics claim abstinence-only programs can teach fear of sex, and that they perpetuate the ignorance, secrecy, and implicit shame of human sexuality. Experts believe that scaring kids away from sexually transmitted diseases and making sex shameful is a bad introduction to healthy sex. The only thing abstinence programs teach about condoms is the failure rate, which they sometimes exaggerate.

Critics also say that abstinence-only programs do not prepare students for safe sex. Supporters of the programs say: If you are going to be abstinent, why learn about contraception? But sometimes sex happens without planning. And it may happen without contraception. This is especially true when there is a mistaken belief that a girl can't get pregnant the first time she has sex. According to one report, 26 percent of females who report abstinence as their regular method of birth control become pregnant each year.

The National Education Association (NEA) and many other organizations have joined the National Coalition against Censorship in a statement against abstinence-only education for restricting students' access to information. Some taxpayers have even challenged the legality of school abstinence-only programs. They claim that withholding information about pregnancy and disease prevention is irresponsible.

Some programs have been legally challenged because they use government funding for abstinence-only programs that are said to include religious activities and promote religious messages.

The American Civil Liberties Union (ACLU) challenged the Louisiana Governor's Program on Abstinence in November 2004 because the ACLU claimed that the religious content of a Web program violated the separation of church and state. The program advised readers: "Abstaining from sex until entering a loving marriage will make you really, truly 'cool' in God's eyes." About a year later, a Louisiana court refused to hold the Governor's Program on Abstinence in contempt for continuing to preach with taxpayer dollars. In 2005, the ACLU filed a lawsuit against the U.S. Department of Health and Human Services, claiming that the federal government improperly used funds to promote religion in an abstinence-only program. In response to this, the Silver Ring Thing, an international teen abstinence group that holds presentations in dozens of cities, quickly modified its program. It removed overtly religious messages from its website, and added a different version of its 12-step program for those who do not want the religious version. The ACLU and its supporters claim that such legal challenges help to keep abstinence-only programs medically accurate, and free of gender and religious bias.

Abstinence programs attempt to delay the age of sexual intercourse, and they succeed in many cases. But how many pledges are broken? Some experts claim that pledge takers who break their pledges are less likely to use condoms than those who never pledged. Certainly, abstinence does not work for those who break pledges, and some critics suggest that pledges break more often than condoms.

## Abstinence-Only and World AIDS Day

On World AIDS Day on December 1, 2004, many AIDS workers were critical of the abstinence-only approach. Some of them said that it was often ineffective at lowering pregnancy rates, and it was a threat to human life because it did not teach people how to prevent the spread of AIDS. This is especially true in Africa, where there is widespread gender inequality. In Zambia, for example, most women are afraid to ask their husbands to use condoms, even if they know their husbands may be infected with HIV.

*A worker from the United Nations teaches women in Cambodia about the importance of using condoms to prevent AIDS and other STDs.*

The program known as ABC, in which A stands for Abstinence, B for Be faithful, and C for Condom use—if the partners are not in a faithful marriage, or if the first two fail—has been introduced to a number of countries in Africa. Sean Healy, spokesman for Doctors Without Borders, talked about the ABC approach on World AIDS Day. He said it might sound good in theory, but in practice it was often prone to ineffective moralizing. ABC was jeered by activists at the global AIDS conference. It was blasted as unworkable in countries where women face forced sex with husbands who have been infected by prostitutes, where young girls are coerced into sex by older men, and young people are sexually active with many partners. The ABC program was called a serious setback to the AIDS control effort; however, it appears to have been successful in Uganda.

## Abstinence in Uganda

The ABC campaign is credited with playing a large part in reducing the number of people with AIDS in Uganda, the country in Africa that has been most successful at confronting this widespread disease. Uganda is a poor, war-torn nation that reduced its national HIV infection rate from about 21 percent to 6 percent, according to the National Heritage Foundation.

There is controversy about how much credit for the reduction of AIDS should go to abstinence programs and how much to increased condom use. According to Steven Sinding of International Planned Parenthood, condom use rose from 2 percent in 1989 to 59 percent in 2003. Certainly, the increased use of condoms played a part for high-risk groups.

The campaign to discourage the behavior that spreads the AIDS virus in Uganda enlisted religious leaders and the popular First Lady of Uganda to aid government officials in spreading the message. Thousands of people were trained to be AIDS counselors and educators in their own communities. Cultural norms about sexual responsibility were preached in churches and mosques. Many people returned to their traditional values of chastity and faithfulness, which they call "zero grazing."

Much of the reduction in AIDS in Uganda is credited to changes in behavior, including increased use of condoms, but reductions in the number of sexual partners likely played the largest role. Even

*The Ugandan government displays anti-AIDS billboards that preach abstinence and fidelity as methods of prevention.*

large numbers of Ugandan teens delayed having sex, and fighting AIDS became a "patriotic duty." There were additional incentives, too, such as testing for HIV with same-day results, and the open discussion of sex and AIDS.

## Teens Speak Out about Abstinence Only

Here are some comments that teens in the United States have made about abstinence-only education:

- "Almost everyone agrees that teens should delay sexual activity until they are married or in a long-term relationship."

- "I think teachers should make sure kids don't fear sex."

- "Everyone has hormones, but abstinence-only courses help me to keep mine under control."

- "Waiting isn't nearly as hard as having a baby or a sexually transmitted disease."

- "The only sure way to avoid sex is to become a hermit."

- "When someone finds making a commitment and sticking with it is unrealistic, it says more about the person's character than about the nature of his or her commitment."

- "Getting pregnant when you don't want to is bad, but sex itself is not bad."

- "The more you tell kids not to have sex, the more they will do it."

- "Abstinence programs can help you stay away from diseases and unexpected pregnancy, but what about the kids in the class who are already sexually active? What about those who break their promises?"

- "Knowledge is power. I want to know more about how to avoid having a baby."

## Is Abstinence for You?

The controversy over abstinence versus safe sex education in the United States continues. While the abstinence-only movement gains momentum in some places, it is losing in others. Many programs are trying to correct the messages of fear and shame that they have been sending to teens. Some experts believe that abstinence-only succeeds for young teens, but not for older ones; and it works for a short time, but not for a long time.

Abstinence means putting off a decision about sex until you believe you have sufficient information, trust, and responsibility to accept the risks that go with it. You have to decide the right time for yourself.

# Chapter 3

# Why Learn about Safe Sex?

Chloe and Nick were in a long-term relationship, one in which friendship turned to love. They shared the same values and beliefs, and they were true to each other. They both had pledged to stay virgins until they were married, and they did just about everything, except have intercourse. Sometimes they would have to say, "No more," to stop themselves from going too far as they struggled with abstinence. Then one time, it just happened. They wondered about an unintended pregnancy.

Chloe and Nick were sure they had nothing to worry about. Chloe had just finished her period, and the chance that she would get pregnant was lower than at other times of the month. Nick said that his sister had used the rhythm method of contraception for years, having intercourse only at times in her menstrual cycle when she would probably not get pregnant. The most dangerous time, the fertile period, is a few days before and after ovulation, which usually occurs fourteen days before the next menstrual period. The few days before that, and the days right after a menstrual period, are the so-called safe times. But timing varies, and in some months fertilization can occur during, right before, or after a menstrual period.

Chloe was worried when her period was late, but she did start to menstruate a week after the expected time. When Chloe went to her doctor, she learned that the lateness could have been due to her worrying about being pregnant. Her doctor told her that even though it was more likely that she would get pregnant at some times than at others, she could get pregnant at any time of the month. Hardly anyone has a completely regular cycle, so it is almost impossible to be certain about avoiding the time of ovulation. Chloe was surprised to learn that she could even get pregnant *during* her period.

If Chloe was going to continue to be sexually active, she would have an 85 percent chance of becoming pregnant within a year if she or her partner did not use contraception. If they wanted to prevent pregnancy, they should learn more about other methods of contraception. The doctor suggested using two methods of birth control at the same time, one of which should be a condom to prevent sexually transmitted diseases. He also told her she should find out if Nick might be carrying an STD.

Chloe was sure Nick had never had sex with another girl, but when she discussed birth control with him he admitted that he had been sexually active before he grew serious about her. Chloe thought she still didn't have to worry because Nick looked healthy, but she learned that many kinds of STDs have no visible symptoms, and people carry them even though they look healthy. Nick had only one instance of unprotected sex with another girl, but one can be all it takes to become infected. Nick promised to go to the local clinic or to his doctor to be tested. If he was positive for any STD, Chloe would need to be tested, too.

Chloe and Nick decided to use contraception for two important reasons. They did not want to be infected with an STD, and they both wanted Chloe to avoid pregnancy. They were seventeen years old and not ready to start a family. Chloe knew something about the responsibilities of teen parents because one of her friends, Adrienne, had a baby when she was sixteen.

## Teen Parenting

Adrienne decided to keep her baby, even though the baby's father didn't want anything to do with her or their son. Her mother promised to care for the baby while Adrienne went to school to earn her high school diploma.

Chloe met Adrienne when the baby was almost a year old. Adrienne loved her son very much, but she was tired all the time. She had to get up at night when the baby cried or was sick. She got up early in the morning to change his diaper and feed him before she went to school. When Adrienne's mother wanted to go out during the school day, or when she was sick, Adrienne had to find someone to stay with her son. Then she worried about how the caregiver handled him. Adrienne felt she was living two lives: one as a mother when she was at home, and another as a teen when she was at school.

Chloe knew Adrienne was missing the parties and the teenage fun that she was enjoying. She wondered if Adrienne would manage to go to college. Like many teen moms, she would probably have to get a low-paying job to help support her son.

Chloe loved babies, but when she saw the challenges Adrienne faced, she was glad she had learned about contraception. She knew she wanted a baby someday, but having a baby before she finished her education was not in her plans.

## Teen Mothers and Fathers Have Special Challenges

Although some teen fathers stay with the mothers, many who had promised marriage before the baby was born leave. Some fathers live with the new family for a while, but find other interests that they decide are more important. Many teen girls who have babies must raise them alone. Some high schools have programs in which teen mothers can take their babies to school and spend time with them between classes and at lunchtime. But most teen mothers have to cut their education short. Only about one-third of teen mothers receive a high school diploma and only 1.5 percent have a college degree by age thirty.

The chance that teen mothers will raise their babies in poverty is high. Eighty-three percent of young women who deliver babies in their teens are poor prior to their pregnancies. Nearly 80 percent of teen mothers go on welfare. And there is a high chance that a very young mother will become pregnant a second time. Even the daughters of teen mothers are likely to become teen mothers themselves, and their sons are 13 percent more likely to end up in prison than those born to older mothers.

Becoming a teen mother poses medical problems, as well. The pelvic bones and birth canals of adolescents are still growing during the teen years, and this increases the risk of complications during vaginal birth. Adolescents are more at risk for prolonged or obstructed labor, which can cause serious long term injuries, so it is especially important for them to have good hospital care.

Medical problems common among adolescent mothers include poor weight gain and pregnancy-induced high blood pressure, a condition that can increase the risk of a heart attack or stroke. Later in life, these mothers are at greater risk of obesity and high blood pressure than women who were not teens when they had their first child. And the poor weight gain of the mother increases the risk of having a low birth-weight baby. Low birth weight raises the probability of infant death, blindness, deafness, mental retardation, chronic respiratory problems, mental illness, and cerebral palsy.

Many teen mothers have been deprived of a supportive home life. Many of them are poor, have suffered physical, emotional, or sexual abuse, receive

*In an effort by the Family Planning Health Services of Wausau, this computer kiosk at North Central Technical College in Wisconsin allows women as young as fifteen to order free condoms and birth control pills.*

inadequate educations, and sense that they have no real future. Two out of five feel stigmatized by their pregnancy and are at greater risk of social isolation and abuse. Many have little or no knowledge of sexuality, prenatal care, and the responsibilities of parenthood. They want a person to love them and believe that having a baby will provide the unconditional love they seek.

Having a baby as a teen is a life-changing experience for fathers, too. Many of them take a responsible part in the life of their child. Counseling helps them understand their feelings and gives them information about their legal rights and responsibilities. Teen fathers have been called the forgotten half of the pregnancy problem. They have the additional strain of financial support for the child. Some have further problems if they want to see their child but the child's mother has moved with the baby to another city.

Preventing teen pregnancy is a highly effective and efficient way to reduce poverty and improve overall child and family well-being. Sex education can help teens postpone the responsibilities that go with pregnancy and teach the importance of avoiding sexually transmitted diseases, some of which may affect their personal health in the teen years, as well as prevent them from having children later in life.

"Teen pregnancy is a tragedy. AIDS is a death sentence," is an oft-quoted statement by a spokeswoman for the Sexuality Information and Education Council of the United States (SIECUS). She says, "The stakes have never been so high."

## How Can You Avoid Sexually Transmitted Diseases?

An important reason for using condoms is the prevention of the spread of some sexually transmitted diseases. Even though a partner looks healthy, he or she may have such a disease. The Centers for Disease

*Condom use is being promoted on billboards across the United States as a way to prevent fatal STDs.*

Control (CDC) estimates that nineteen million STD infections occur annually, almost half of them among young people ages fifteen to twenty-four. Annual testing is recommended for sexually active teens who are not in monogamous relationships. Teens who pledge abstinence need to be tested as soon as they break their pledges. In a study called *After the Promise: The STD Consequences of Adolescent Virginity Pledges,* it was concluded that STD infection rates do not differ among those who do not pledge and those who do, perhaps because those who pledge abstinence are less likely to use condoms at sexual debut and to be tested and diagnosed with STDs. Further studies disagreed with this finding, but since the new studies were based on self-reports, many scientists did not agree with them and believed the earlier studies were more accurate.

Oral sex, which some pledgers deem permissible because they still consider themselves virgins, spreads some of the diseases. Oral and anal sex are ways to prevent pregnancy, but some STDs—such as gonorrhea, herpes, syphilis, and AIDS—can be spread by them.

Emma felt certain she did not have any kind of sexual disease. After all, she had only had sex with Josh, and he was obviously healthy. Emma did not know that Josh had had sex with Ava, and years earlier with Jade. Ava had had sex with Caleb before she met Josh, and Jade had been with Jack. Jack had slept with four other girls. Confusing? The fact is that Emma is vulnerable to any of the diseases any of these people have. Some say that Emma has slept virtually with all of them; at least, she could get a disease from anyone who gave it to Josh.

This series of relationships is not as complicated as the chains of infection map shown in *Time* magazine's February 2005 issue. The map was made by researchers who tried to document all the sexual relationships among students at a high school in a Midwestern town over a period of eighteen months. The researchers made a map that showed how infections could be spread. Most of the students who were sexually active (more than half of them) had had just one or two partners. But 288 of the 832 students who were in the study were in a giant social network. In some cases, even those with one or two partners were at risk of contracting STDs from everyone in the chain of infection. The data were collected using a secure computerized survey, so there was no incentive to lie. It is interesting to note that only about 5 percent of the relationships in this study were hookups for sex only.

Hookups can be a common source of sexually transmitted diseases since many different partners are involved. Lila was a "friend with benefits"—she would hook up with a number of different boys. When Lila had a sore throat, she went to the clinic to see a doctor. She thought she had strep throat, but the doctor insisted on asking questions about her background before he even looked at her throat. Lila insisted she was a virgin. She finally admitted she had oral sex with a number of different partners, but said that was a while ago and she wasn't doing it anymore. When she found out that she had gonorrhea from one of her encounters, she was devastated. "I never did it with anyone who didn't look healthy," she insisted. The doctor told her that many people who are infected have no symptoms. He prescribed antibiotics, which would probably cure Lila's gonorrhea, but she still hated herself for having oral sex. She suffered from depression for several years after the diagnosis.

Since sexually transmitted diseases can cause serious health problems, such as infertility and the increased risk of getting HIV, many teens believe it is worth using condoms. Unfortunately, condoms cannot protect against all STDs. Some teens are not aware of the seriousness of STDs, and some don't even know they exist.

Abstinence from sexual activity or being in a monogamous relationship are the safest ways to avoid STDs. The only way you can be sure you are having safe sex is to keep your partner's blood, semen, or vaginal fluids out of your body and to avoid skin-to-skin contact in the genital area with any person who might have an STD. Laboratory studies have shown that condoms form a barrier to particles the size of the viruses, bacteria, and parasites that cause some of these diseases. But they must be used consistently and correctly.

## Spreading STDs

Since about 65 percent of students in the United States are sexually active by the twelfth grade and one in five has had four or more sexual partners, teenagers are at high risk for STDs. As mentioned earlier, if you are sexually active and any of the sexual partners who came before you had an STD when having unprotected sex, the infection may become yours. Young women are at greater risk of contracting HIV than older women because their cervical cells are less tough than they become later in life.

Twelve-year-old Tina's father comes home drunk every night. On the nights when he has been with a prostitute, he sleeps in his own bed. But some nights he sneaks into Tina's bed and tells her she is his "special" girl. She doesn't like being his special girl, but she is afraid to tell her mother that her father has sex with her. Her father tells Tina she is too young to get pregnant since her periods haven't started. He thinks he does not need contraception. This is not true. Girls can become pregnant even before they start to menstruate. It is true that by not using a condom, he is infecting her with his gonorrhea.

In some countries, where men believe having sex with a virgin is a cure for their own sexually transmitted diseases, and where young girls accept unprotected sex from older men in order to pay for school or food for their families, many young girls become infected. Since many of the old men believe that young girls are pure, they don't wear condoms.

Even husbands spread STDs to their wives if they have been infected by other women and don't use condoms. In some countries in Africa, where women are taught never to refuse sex with their husbands, many men don't wear condoms even if they know they are infected. And it is not considered acceptable for the wives to ask them to do so. In developed countries,

*An HIV-positive AIDS educator in South Africa speaks with a resident about safe sex. Part of her goal is to do away with the stigma associated with the disease within their community.*

most women can and do play a part in contraception.

For most sexually active American teens, the use of condoms is an important factor in the protection against unwanted pregnancy and sexually transmitted diseases. The CDC acknowledges that condoms are effective against the spread of HIV, an incurable condition that usually leads to AIDS and requires extensive medical treatment. By 2005, more than forty million people worldwide were infected with HIV. In Africa, more than twenty-five million were infected and 6,500 people were dying each day from diseases that their weakened immune systems could no longer fight. Condom use and abstinence are being promoted to prevent the spread of AIDS in Africa, but more than twenty-five million people may die from it by 2025. Since 2002, the CDC has deemphasized its support for condom use in favor of abstinence in all countries, but the value of condom use in disease prevention has been demonstrated in many areas. For example, in Thailand, condoms are credited with dramatically reducing HIV/AIDS. They reversed the course of the epidemic in a relatively short time.

In the United States, AIDS still makes the headlines, especially as an increasing number of women are becoming sick. At first, AIDS was spread among men having sex with men—where, still, the largest group of people are infected—and those who were infected by contaminated needles. Then it spread through bisexual men to their female partners. Women can infect their babies at birth.

Although AIDS has been recognized since 1981 as a disease that destroys the immune system, many young people do not realize that a person may be infected with HIV and can spread it, even though there are no symptoms. Symptoms of HIV infection may not occur for days, weeks, months, or years after infection. Condoms reduce the risk of HIV/AIDS, gonorrhea, chlamydia, and trichomoniasis, diseases that are described on pages 51–53. Talk to a health-care provider if you think you might have been exposed.

If you have an unusual discharge, skin irritation, or itch in the genital area, call the CDC National STD Hotline for further information and testing sites. Your health-care provider can help you decide what tests you need.

English: 1-800-227-8922; available 24 hours a day, 7 days a week

Spanish: 1-800-344-7432; available 8 A.M. to 2 A.M. EST, 7 days a week

TYY for hearing impaired: 1-800-243-7889; available Monday through Friday, 10 A.M. to 10 P.M. EST

National AIDS Hotline:

English: 1-800-342-2437

Spanish: 1-800-344-7432

TYY: 1-800-243-7889

# Information about Some Common STDs

| STD | Cause | How it's spread | Symptoms | Treatment |
|-----|-------|-----------------|----------|-----------|
| **Chancroid** | bacteria | skin-to-skin contact with an open sore | genital sores | antibiotics |
| **Chlamydia** | bacteria | during vaginal, anal, or oral sex; probably most common STD in America | may have no symptoms; can cause PID and sterility | antibiotics |
| **Crabs (pubic lice)** | parasites | contact with pubic or other hair and clothing of infected people | itching | over-the-counter medication |
| **Gonorrhea** | bacteria | sexual contact; contact with bodily fluids | genital pain, penile or vaginal discharge, sore throat, joint pains; can cause PID and sterility | antibiotics |

# Information about Some Common STDs

| STD | Cause | How it's spread | Symptoms | Treatment |
|-----|-------|-----------------|----------|-----------|
| **Hepatitis B** | virus | sexual contact and infected needles; vaccination available and now mandatory in some states before 8th grade | yellow skin and eyes, fatigue, dark urine, light stools; may have no symptoms | no treatment available |
| **Genital herpes** | virus | skin-to-skin and mucus-to-skin contact | painful, itchy blisters or sores on the penis, vagina, mouth, anus, or skin; swollen glands, muscle aches, fever; recurs intermittently | control with antiviral drugs; no cure |
| **HIV/AIDS** | virus | contact of infected sexual discharges and blood with mucous membranes in mouth, vagina, rectum | fever, fatigue, weight loss, infections, diarrhea, night sweats; symptoms may not appear for up to 10 years | control with antiviral drugs; no cure |

| STD | Cause | How it's spread | Symptoms | Treatment |
|---|---|---|---|---|
| **Genital warts (HPV)** | virus | intimate body contact | itching and irritation; bumps (warts) around penis, vagina, or anus; may lead to cervical cancer in women | removal of warts by freezing or burning |
| **Syphilis** | bacteria | skin contact during sexual activity | painless sores on penis, vagina, mouth, or anus, followed by fever, joint pain, or rash; can cause serious heart, brain, or nerve disease | antibiotics |
| **Trichomoniasis** | protozoa | sexual activity | usually none in men; women may have smelly, foamy, yellow, green, or gray vaginal discharge | Metronidazole, a prescription drug |

# Chapter 4

## Secret Lives of Teens

### Erica

One Monday night, fifteen-year-old Erica received a phone call that she would never forget. It was Matt, her boyfriend, whose voice sounded shaky and scared as he told her he thought she should get tested for chlamydia, the most common sexually transmitted disease in the United States. Matt said he became worried when he heard that his previous girlfriend was infected, and he thought that he and Erica should both be tested. Erica was panicked because she and Matt did not use a condom the one and only time they had sex. They weren't prepared because they hadn't really planned to have intercourse. What would she do if she was infected? At least she was thankful that she wasn't pregnant. She didn't want to tell her parents; they didn't even know she had a boyfriend. She felt guilty and ashamed. Maybe chlamydia was punishment for having sex.

Erica thought her parents were very old-fashioned and overprotective. They didn't want her to go out with boys, and had never even discussed sex with her. They believed that avoiding any talk about sex would keep her innocent and pure. Erica attended a religious school where the sex education classes emphasized the importance of abstinence until marriage and provided very little information about contraception. She was taught that sex before marriage was sinful, and that masturbating or even having sexual fantasies was wrong. She felt guilty for having sexual feelings. Nobody had told her that it was perfectly normal for young people to experience these feelings. When she started dating Matt, she already felt like a slut.

Matt's news made Erica feel anxious and depressed. Her parents noticed the change in her mood, and it was clear that she would have to tell them what was troubling her. She knew she needed help. When she finally told them, her parents were upset to learn that their daughter was not as innocent as they had hoped, but they didn't call her a whore or throw her out of the house, as Erica had feared. They were concerned because she still felt confused and depressed, even after she received the good news that Matt was not infected with chlamydia.

Erica's parents weren't comfortable talking about sex, but they realized that it was important for her to discuss the issues that were troubling her. They consulted a psychiatrist who specialized in treating the problems of teenagers; he helped Erica and her parents talk more openly about sex. Erica realized that she had indulged in risky behavior, but that it didn't make her a bad person. Erica's parents realized that they couldn't stop her from growing up and that it wasn't abnormal or bad for teenagers to have sexual desires. They learned that knowing about sex helps teenagers make better decisions.

## Zeke

Zeke hated going into the boys' locker room at his high school because the other guys were always boasting about the size of their penises and about their success in getting girls to have sex with them. Zeke was a good-looking, muscular football player, and the girls in his class thought he was cool, but he was shy around them. Zeke wasn't ready to date them.

At Christmas, he was invited to a party where many of the older boys and girls were drinking and no parents were there to supervise. Against his better judgment, Zeke was persuaded to join in the drinking, and he downed a few glasses of punch that made him very relaxed and sleepy. He went upstairs to the bedroom where he had left his jacket, and feeling a bit dizzy from the alcohol, decided to take a rest on the bed. He woke up to find a naked girl in the bed undressing him. At first, he was angry, but she managed to seduce him. After some foreplay, they had intercourse. He never saw the girl again, but he overcame his shyness around girls. After his first experience, Zeke changed his attitude about girls. He really liked them, but mostly for sex. He never developed a good or long-term relationship with a girl, but he had sexual encounters with many of them. Now he joined in talking about sex with the boys in the locker room. Zeke thought he was a prize to girls, but he had no idea what real love was all about.

## Connor

Connor felt that he was different from other boys since third grade, but he didn't know why. He never thought of himself as gay until he reached seventh grade when most of his friends were becoming interested in girls. Connor just didn't have any interest in girls, but eventually he realized he *was* attracted to boys. It was then that he realized he was homosexual. Connor felt he didn't fit in with his friends, but he kept his feelings secret.

When Connor's classmates teased him about being different, he felt as if he had done something wrong. He spent a lot of time just sitting and staring into space. After some taunts about AIDS, Connor secretly wondered if he would eventually die from AIDS. He knew that not all gays had AIDS, but he thought someday he might be one of them who did.

Coming to terms with his sexual orientation, together with deciding whether to come out to friends and family, was a great crisis in Connor's life. This was a huge secret, especially since his parents made nasty remarks about gays once in a while. Would he be a family outcast if they knew?

The feelings of isolation and loneliness that come with being different at a time in life when it is so important to fit in can be almost unbearable. Connor made an appointment with the school counselor. He would share his secret with her, and sometime in the future he might be able to share it with those close to him.

## Nadia

When they were in their second year of high school, fifteen-year-old Nadia and her boyfriend, Ramon, made a commitment to remain virgins until marriage. They belonged to a group whose members had all signed abstinence pledges, and they were sure that they could keep their promise. However, as the year went by, they were finding it more and more difficult to refrain from intercourse. Then one evening, it finally happened.

Because they hadn't planned it, they didn't have a condom or any other kind of protection. One of Nadia's friends who wasn't in the program carried a condom in her purse when she went out with her boyfriend, even though they weren't planning to have sex. But Nadia believed that carrying protection means you really do intend to have intercourse. The abstinence-only program hadn't provided much information about birth control methods. To her horror, Nadia realized that it was the tenth day of her menstrual cycle, a time when there was a very real chance of pregnancy even though Ramon had withdrawn before ejaculation.

Nadia thought about what she would do if she was

pregnant. Abortion wasn't an option for her. Going through a pregnancy and then letting a couple adopt the baby would be difficult. But she and Ramon were too young to become parents. They both wanted to go to college, and having a baby would ruin their plans for the future.

Nadia's mother wondered why her daughter seemed unusually irritable and moody during the next two weeks, but Nadia couldn't summon up the courage to confide in her. When Nadia's period arrived, she was finally relieved of her anxiety, but she was angry with herself and Ramon for having acted so carelessly. They both felt guilty for breaking the abstinence pledge, and they felt really stupid for having unprotected sex. They had been lucky this time. It wasn't going to happen again.

Nadia and Ramon kept their secret, but it had been a very difficult time, especially because they didn't seek advice from their parents. They were afraid that their parents would react with anger and disappointment, forbid them to see each other again, and ground them forever. In reality, their parents were understanding and probably would have given them the support they needed if they had shared their secret. Like many teens, Ramon and Nadia had trouble voicing their concerns about sex and asking for help. This is especially true since some abstinence-only education programs block inform-ation about safe sex from many teens.

For those who are already sexually active, inform-ation about safe sex can be a matter of life or death. For example, most teens don't know that about 25 percent of the estimated one million people in the

United States who are living with HIV are unaware that they are infected. So it is quite possible for teens to infect each other without knowing it.

Some teens think that they need not worry about HIV since there are drugs to treat AIDS. "If I get it, I'll just take the medicine," has been the comment of a number of teens. But the medicine does not cure the disease, and a great deal of suffering accompanies treatment.

Many teens like those discussed earlier have secret lives that can lead to serious problems. There is no 100 percent safe sex, except for people who are in committed, monogamous relationships. If you have any kind of sex-related problem, or even if you are just thinking about becoming sexually active, you don't have to wrestle with questions alone; it's always more helpful to seek information, advice, or support from a parent, doctor, counselor, or other trusted adult.

Counselors and doctors are legally obligated to remain confidential. Even though this is true, many teens feel more comfortable if they pretend to be asking for advice on behalf of a friend. Just talking about the problem helps them to sort out the facts. Sometimes this prevents actions that teens regret later.

# Chapter 5

# Where You Can Learn about Safe Sex

Marcy, like many sixteen-year-olds, learned about contraception from her friends. They told her that if she douched—washed out her vagina—with Coca-Cola, she would not get pregnant. But no kind of douching is an effective method of birth control because the sperm that were deposited during intercourse have already had time to travel to an egg.

Some of Marcy's friends believed they couldn't get pregnant if they were standing when they had sex. Sperm can easily travel up a woman's vagina no matter what position she is in. Standing while having intercourse is not a form of birth control; nor is standing during intercourse in a swimming pool.

Several of Marcy's friends thought they would not get pregnant if a boy withdrew before he had an orgasm, when he ejaculates releasing millions of sperm. This is not a reliable way to prevent pregnancy since a small amount of sperm is released before ejaculation. It takes just one sperm to fertilize an egg and begin a pregnancy, and there are thousands of sperm in the small amount of fluid that is released before ejaculation.

## Parents as Sex Educators

You would probably do better talking about birth control with your parents than with your friends. Even though parents may not know all the answers or be sympathetic, they are usually much better sources of reliable information than friends. In some families, parents begin sex education when their child is a few years old by answering questions honestly, but not including information that is inappropriate for the child's age. They help their children understand themselves as sexual human beings. Many parents would rather talk with their children honestly than have them learn about sex from others who may be less knowledgeable.

About 70 percent of teens, both boys and girls, discuss sex with their parents, although they prefer to do it casually rather than to have a formal discussion. Although most parents hope their children will be abstinent until marriage, some of them are willing to talk with their children about contraception and/or help them get medical advice. Almost half the teens in one study said that parents influence their decisions about sex more strongly than friends, teachers, and others. Eighty-eight percent of teens say it would be easier to postpone sexual activity and avoid teen pregnancy if they were able to have more open, honest conversations about these topics with their parents.

Although parents are the source of information that is most helpful to many teens, some parents are uncomfortable discussing sex. Even when parents talk with their kids about sex, there may be questions that remain unanswered.

## Sex Education in Schools

Does your school have an abstinence-only program? Do you know anybody who wants more information about abstinence? While some claim that abstinence

*Sex education in schools varies from teaching abstinence-only to teaching effective methods of contraception. Young people don't always get all the information they need in order to make an informed decision. Parents, counselors, doctors, and family planning clinics are good alternatives.*

is 100 percent safe, this is true only when it is practiced 100 percent of the time. For most teens, abstinence is the best answer for their sexual health, but many teens don't choose abstinence. If you have an abstinence-only program in your school and you think you might be sexually active before you are married, try talking with parents, a teacher, a counselor, your doctor, a religious leader, or visit a family planning clinic, which is described later in this chapter.

In 2001, Dr. David Satcher, who was then surgeon general of the United States, issued a report that recommended mature and thoughtful discussion of sexuality in schools. The report says that adults can trust young people with messages that say, "If you are sexually active, this is how you protect yourself." It endorses abstinence as the best strategy to help teens avoid unwanted pregnancy and sexually transmitted diseases, but says education on safe sex and contraception is also needed. "Persons of all ages and backgrounds are at risk [of unwanted pregnancy and sexually transmitted diseases] and should have access to knowledge and social services necessary for optimal sexual health. . . . To have people not be aware of how to best protect themselves when sexually active is just not fair," Dr. Satcher said.

The majority of parents and teachers welcome sex education in schools, preferring that abstinence is taught as the best method of contraception, but with information about birth control for those who are already sexually active and those who become sexually active before they are ready for pregnancy. As far back as 1970, numerous surveys showed that more than half of adults approved of sex education classes that included information about birth control. By 2003, the vast majority of parents in the United States supported comprehensive, medically accurate sex education. Seventy-five percent wanted their children to receive information on condom use, sexually transmitted diseases, safe sex practices, communication, coping skills, and the emotional aspects of sexual relationships. Today, about one-third of American high schools have sex education programs that teach abstinence until marriage as the way to avoid pregnancy and sexually transmitted diseases, but provide no information about birth control or preventing infections.

## Family Planning Clinics

A nationwide network of 4,600 clinics in the United States that are supported by a federal program known as Title X provide reproductive services to five million people each year. Some of these people are teens. Planned Parenthood is the most well-known family planning clinic. The Planned Parenthood website gives information on clinics in your area that provide contraception.

Some clinics are located in a state or local health department, hospital, or university health center, and some are located independently. Recently in the United States, 917,000 girls under the age of eighteen obtained family planning services at federally funded clinics. Some of these services included prescription contraception, information, and counseling. Doctors and phone books are good ways to find the location of a clinic.

# Sex and Television

No matter what you learn about sex in school, you learn more about sex when you watch television. If you, like the average teen, watch three hours of television a day, you are exposed to some heavy doses of sexual content. Think about the last television drama you watched. Did it depict some sexual activity? Chances are that it did, since two out of every three shows include sexual content. Daytime soaps are famous for depicting casual sex. But did you learn anything from these programs about contraception?

In the thousands of sexual references on television in one year, contraception was mentioned only about 175 times. The popular sitcom *Friends* is famous for the scene in which one of the characters discussed her unexpected pregnancy. When she informed the father that she was pregnant, he was surprised because he had worn a condom. From this episode, many viewers remembered—or learned for the first time—that condoms are not 100 percent effective, even when used properly. Condoms are 97 percent effective when used properly, but some viewers remembered only the failure. The majority of teens who watched the show continued to think of condoms as somewhat, or very, effective. The RAND Corporation, which contacted many viewers after this episode, noted that a large proportion of teens talked with a parent or other adult about the effectiveness of condoms as a result of watching it.

Television has a strong effect on the sexual behavior of teens. Surveys have shown that many teens find television portrayals of sexual issues to be accurate reflections of real-world experiences and outcomes. For as many as one in five teens, entertainment is reported to be their most important source of sexual information. But what they see and hear about sex on TV is often misleading, distorted, and incomplete. Casual sex between unmarried people is depicted as acceptable, and often without risks and consequences. When viewers have intense reactions to entertainment, it enhances learning, so it's easy to learn behavior from television that puts your health at risk.

A study by the RAND Corporation found that teens who watch a lot of TV with sexual content are twice as likely as their peers to begin engaging in sexual intercourse in the following year. Do you think it makes a difference whether you watch a show in which people talk about sex or one in which they are shown having sex? The RAND study found that both affect teens' perception of what is normal sexual behavior and propels their own sexual behavior.

Even though television programming is a popular source of information about sexual behavior, the commercials on television that deal with male sexual arousal are far more common than those about birth control. In spite of these provocative ads about sexual arousal, comparatively few commercials about contraception are aired. The first ad for condoms to appear in prime time was aired June 1, 2005, on NBC and WB, and ads for female contraception became more frequent around that time. Some programs on television provide helpful information. Since 1997, MTV and the Kaiser Family Foundation have partnered on Emmy award-winning educational programs to inform and empower young people about critical sexual health issues. Programs such as *The 411: Teens & Sex,* give teens and their parents an environment in which to talk with each other about sex, a subject that is often difficult for them to approach. This program, shown January 26, 2005, as an hour-long news special on NBC, was hosted by Katie Couric in a relaxed vacation setting where parents in a separate room were given a chance to discuss some of their thoughts on the subject of teens and sex.

Although TV is a strong influence, it is not the only factor affecting teens' decisions to have sex. In fact, many teens say that TV makes sex look unimportant, just recreational, and not a very serious subject. Education, good mental health religion, and parental influence may help young people resist the unrealistic situations presented on television and help them make better and more informed decisions. Public-service announcements, especially about the use of condoms to protect against disease, have reached millions of people.

## Music and Music Videos

Song lyrics also convey messages about sex. Whether it's a song that tells you to enjoy sex without concern for the consequences, or one that makes sex a violent act used to degrade women, lyrics are full of sex. Superstars sing about everything from rough sex to safe sex. As with television, many lyrics portray sexual messages that are unrealistic and inaccurate, a far cry from what teens need to know in order to have a healthy adolescence, whether they opt for abstinence or another form of birth control. Some teens say they enjoy the music and don't listen to the words in which singers objectify women with their lyrics.

Many hip-hop videos show women scantily clad as sex toys, and one even portrays them as appliances. The hip-hop culture has become more sexist than when it started in the 1970s. As a result, many African-American women are fighting back in a campaign called "Take Back the Music," sponsored by *Essence*, a magazine for black women with a circulation of more than 1.6 million.

## The Internet

The Internet is the source of an overwhelming amount of information about sex. Some of it is educational, and some of it is explicit, inaccurate, and/or distasteful. Teens can be exposed to this kind of material either because they search for it or because it comes to them as spam. Many parents prefer to keep this away from young people, using house rules and Internet filters that prevent access to material they think is unsuitable.

On the other hand, many educational articles, videos, and other information about the media and sex education can be found by searching the Web. These are especially plentiful in May of each year when the National Campaign to Prevent Teen Pregnancy sponsors the National Day to Prevent Teen Pregnancy Quiz (<http://www.teenpregnancy.org>). At that time, you can participate in National Quiz Day along with hundreds of thousands of other teens.

Some other valuable sites that provide information about pregnancy prevention and how to avoid sexually transmitted diseases are listed on pages 117–118.

## Other Media

Billboards, posters, magazine articles, and flyers with messages promoting abstinence or providing information about safe sex seem to be increasing in number. You can learn about contraception in doctors' offices, from religious advisers, and through other counselors. This information may add to what you find in this and other books listed on pages 115–116.

# Chapter 6

# How Your Sex Organs Work

If you are between the ages of ten and fourteen, you've probably noticed that you have begun to undergo some dramatic changes. Girls and boys experience a growth spurt and may grow several inches in a year. Boys become more muscular, their voices deepen, and their penises and testes get bigger. Girls gain weight around the hips, and their breasts begin to develop. Hair sprouts under the arms and in the pubic area around the genitals. Many teens get acne. This is the time of life known as puberty, and it may occur as early as age eight or as late as age fifteen.

# What's Happening in Your Body?

Puberty starts when special cells in your brain begin producing a chemical called gonadotrophin-releasing hormone (GnRH). GnRH acts on the anterior pituitary gland, a small gland just below the brain, triggering the manufacture of two other hormones: luteinizing hormone (LH) and follicle-stimulating hormone (FSH). LH and FSH target the sex organs of both boys and girls. In boys, these hormones stimulate the production of sperm and the male sex hormone testosterone. In girls, they stimulate the maturation of eggs and the production of estrogen and progesterone, the female sex hormones.

Long before puberty, before you were born, your sex organs began to take shape. Early in its development, each embryo starts out with two pairs of structures: the Wolffian ducts and the Mullerian ducts. If the embryo is female, the Wolffian ducts disappear and the Mullerian ducts develop into the female sex organs. If the embryo is male, the Mullerian ducts disappear and the Wolffian ducts develop into the male sex organs.

From a biological point of view, the main object of the sex organs is to produce a new individual by combining two sets of genetic material, one from the female and one from the male. This process—fusion of the sperm and egg—is called fertilization. In some organisms, fertilization takes place outside the body without any contact between male and female. For example, a female fish lays her eggs at the bottom of a lake, and then a male deposits his sperm on them. But mammals use a system that has a better chance of

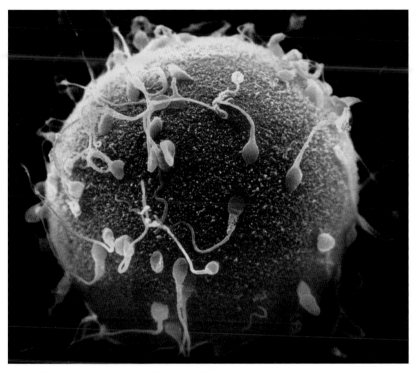

*Males release some 300 million sperm that travel through the uterus to reach and fertilize the female's one egg. Only a few hundred sperm survive the journey to encounter the egg, and only one sperm actually fertilizes it.*

producing offspring: The male deposits his sperm inside the female, where fertilization takes place. Male and female sex organs are specially designed to perform this function of internal fertilization.

## Male Sex Organs

A boy's penis and testes (also called testicles) are the parts of the male reproductive system that are visible

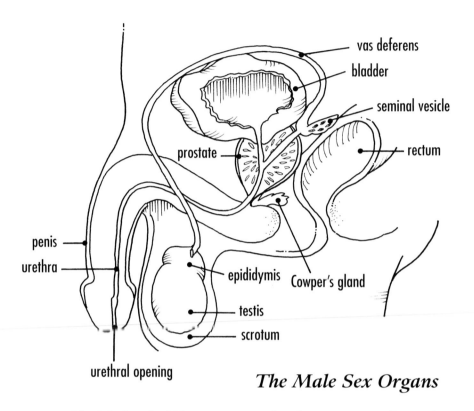

vas deferens

bladder

seminal vesicle

rectum

prostate

penis

urethra

epididymis   Cowper's gland

testis

scrotum

urethral opening

*The Male Sex Organs*

outside his body. The testes make the sperm cells and the male sex hormone testosterone. Testosterone is responsible for secondary sex characteristics such as facial hair, typical male body shape, muscular development, and voice tone.

The main part of the penis is known as the shaft and at the end is the glans. The foreskin is a piece of skin that covers the glans and can be slid back. Sometimes boys have their foreskin removed at birth, a procedure called circumcision.

The wrinkly sac of skin that hangs down behind the penis is called the scrotum, and it contains the testes. (The singular is testis.) They are located outside the body because sperm cells need a temperature that is lower than the normal body temperature in order to develop properly.

Inside each testis are many feet of tiny coiled tubules where the sperm are made. The sperm cells are then transported to another series of coiled tubes, the epididymis, where they mature and are stored. During sexual intercourse, the sperm travel through a tube inside the body called the vas deferens. Secretions from the prostate gland, seminal vesicles, and Cowper's glands are mixed with the sperm along the way. This mixture is the seminal fluid, or semen. It passes through another tube, the urethra, leading into the penis, and exits during ejaculation. The urethra in males has two functions. In addition to serving as a passageway for sperm, it carries urine from the bladder through the penis to the outside of the body, but a valve prevents urine from mixing with sperm.

## Female Sex Organs

While a boy's main sex organs—the penis and testes—are located outside his body, a girl's sex organs are inside her body. The main female sex organs where sex cells are formed are called ovaries. They are small oval organs that are located on either side of the uterus, a muscular organ that has the shape and size of an upside-down pear.

Unlike a boy, a girl is born with hundreds of sex cells, called eggs, already present in her ovaries. When she reaches puberty, the eggs complete their development and are released once a month. This process is known as ovulation. At puberty, the ovaries also start

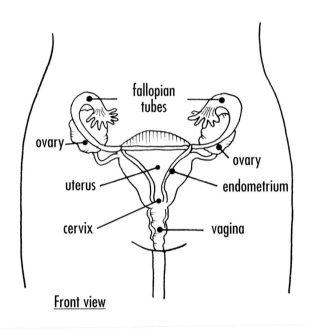

fallopian
tubes

ovary

ovary

uterus

endometrium

cervix

vagina

Front view

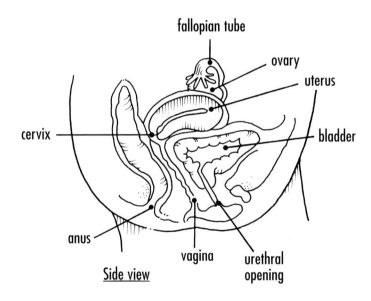

fallopian tube

ovary

uterus

cervix

bladder

anus

vagina

urethral
opening

Side view

*The Female Sex Organs*

76

manufacturing the female sex hormone estrogen, which is responsible for the secondary sex characteristics such as breast development and pubic hair. The ovaries also manufacture the hormone progesterone and some testosterone, the male sex hormone.

The fallopian tubes, or oviducts, are paired tubes that lead into the uterus. At the bottom end of the uterus is a structure called the cervix that leads into the vagina. At the end of the vagina are two sets of folded skin called the labia, which cover the opening of the vagina to the outside. Also on the outside is the clitoris, a sensitive pea-sized structure, which is the remainder of the embryonic Wolffian ducts that would have developed into a penis in a boy.

In contrast to boys, the urinary system in girls has no connection to the sex organs. Urine flows from the bladder into the urethra and out through a separate opening. The opening of the vagina is between the opening of the urethra in front and the end of the digestive tract (anus) in back.

Partially covering the opening of the vagina is a thin membrane called the hymen. A girl is considered a virgin if her hymen has not been stretched or torn by sexual intercourse. If a girl's hymen is no longer intact because she uses tampons, plays sports, or engages in gymnastics, it doesn't mean she is not a virgin. In some cultures, having an intact hymen as a sign of virginity is so important that some women undergo an operation to reconstruct a torn hymen.

Every month an egg is released, popping through the surface of the ovary, entering into the opening of the fallopian tube and from there traveling to the uterus. After an egg is released, the lining of the uterus becomes thickened to prepare for the arrival of a fertilized egg. If the egg is not fertilized, the lining of the uterus sheds about fourteen days after ovulation; shedding tissue and blood is the process known as menstruation.

If a woman has intercourse while the egg is still in the fallopian tube and she isn't using any form of birth control, she can become pregnant. Sperm swim from the vagina up through the opening in the cervix, through the uterus, and into the fallopian tubes. Here is where fertilization occurs if a sperm joins the egg. Millions of sperm are released in the semen, and only a small number reach the fallopian tubes. But only one sperm fertilizes the egg. In that case, the lining of the uterus doesn't shed, but remains thick in order to receive the fertilized egg, which starts its growth as it travels down the fallopian tube to the uterus, where it becomes implanted and develops into a baby.

## What Happens During Sex?

When people become sexually excited, their heart rate increases, they breathe more rapidly, they become warm, and they secrete fluids that lubricate their sexual organs. The penis and the clitoris contain a special kind of spongy tissue called erectile tissue, which has the ability to swell up with blood. Stimulation of these parts of the body provides very pleasurable sensations.

When a man is sexually aroused, his brain sends messages to blood vessels in the erectile tissue, causing more blood to flow in through the small arteries than out through the veins. The increased amount of blood makes the penis expand and get hard. This makes it possible for him to insert his penis into the woman's vagina. Women secrete lubrication to assist in the penetration of the penis. As sexual excitement builds up, contractions in the vas deferens, prostate, and seminal vesicles propel semen from the penis into the vagina; this is known as ejaculation, informally known as coming. Then the male's veins open up, allowing blood to flow out normally again, and the penis shrinks and becomes soft. The same thing happens to the erectile tissue in a woman's clitoris, although it isn't as noticeable. As a result, stimulation of the clitoris can lead to orgasm.

Most teens have a lot of questions and concerns about their bodies and sex, and what's normal and what isn't. Listed at the end of this book are numerous information sources—books, hotlines, organizations, and websites—where you can find answers to almost any question you might have.

# Chapter 7

# What You Should Know about Contraception

Maybe you have chosen abstinence because you know that the only 100 percent sure way of avoiding pregnancy and sexually transmitted diseases is to avoid sex 100 percent of the time. Most teenagers, including those who have had sex, think that teens should wait until they are older before engaging in sex. So why learn about other means of protection? Because even people committed to remaining abstinent can break the pledge.

According to the U.S. Department of Health and Human Services, 82 percent of all teen pregnancies are unintended. Each year, one out of every ten teenagers between the ages of fifteen and nineteen gets pregnant. In a nationwide survey of twelve thousand teenagers between the ages of twelve and eighteen, it was found that 88 percent of those who had pledged abstinence reported that they later had sexual intercourse before marriage. Teens who pledged virginity married earlier, had fewer partners, and delayed sexual intercourse by an average of about eighteen months longer than those who did not take the pledge. However, the teens who had pledged abstinence were much less likely to use condoms the first time they had sex, and they were less likely to have been tested for STDs. The rate of STDs was about the same for pledgers and non-pledgers.

By age twenty-four, one of every three sexually active people will have a sexually transmitted disease, so you can see it is important to know how to protect yourself from pregnancy and STDs before you become sexually active. If you choose to be sexually active and are informed, you can avoid becoming part of these statistics. Here's what you need to know:

There are many different methods of contraception, and some are better than others for preventing pregnancy. Whatever method you choose has to be used correctly, and it has to be used every time you have sex. Partners need to be faithful to each other and not have sex with anyone else in order to reduce the chance of giving or getting an STD. As mentioned earlier, the latex condom is the only contraceptive method that can provide protection against most STDs, including HIV/AIDS. Whether you are straight or gay, you can guard against infection. Without a condom, infections can be passed from one person to another during vaginal, anal, or oral sex. But even condoms may not be effective against some STDs, such as human papillomavirus (HPV), the virus that causes genital warts and may lead to cervical cancer.

## Barrier Methods

These methods prevent sperm from reaching the egg:

### Male Condom ("Rubber")

Condoms are latex sheaths that are placed over the erect penis to collect the semen. Although they are not 100 percent failure-proof, they are very effective for preventing pregnancy and some STDs. You don't need a prescription to buy condoms. They are readily available in pharmacies and supermarkets, and there are many brands to choose from. For people who are allergic to rubber, there are polyurethane condoms. Lambskin condoms are not recommended because

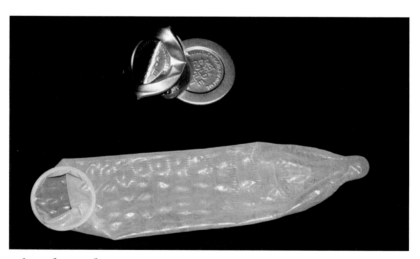

*A male condom*

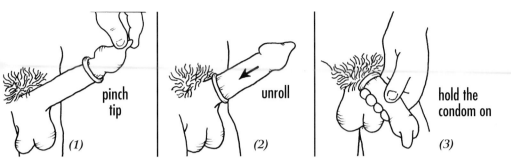

pinch
tip

*(1)*

unroll

*(2)*

hold the
condom on

*(3)*

*How to use a male condom: (1) Place the condom on
the end of the penis and pinch the tip of the condom,
(2) unroll the condom until it covers the entire length
of the penis, (3) hold the condom on until after ejaculation
and while withdrawing from your partner, then remove
the condom from the penis.*

they have tiny pores that can allow the transmission of infections. It's important to follow the directions on the package. Condoms shouldn't be used past the expiration date, and they should be discarded if they look dry or brittle. If you use a lubricant, it should be water-based, because oil-containing lubricants such as petroleum jelly can weaken latex. A condom should be rolled down over the erect penis, with a half-inch of space left at the end for the semen. After ejaculation, the penis should be withdrawn carefully, holding the condom so that the semen does not leak out.

If a girl performs oral sex on a boy, he should always use a condom. If a boy performs oral sex on a girl, a cut-up condom or a dental dam should be used as a barrier between the mouth and genitals. A dental dam is a piece of latex that dentists sometimes place in your mouth to keep fluids or other material from getting down your throat.

## Female Condom

This is a thin polyurethane sheath that is placed inside the vagina before sex, with a soft ring inside that holds it in place covering the vagina and cervix. It collects the semen and prevents it from entering the vagina. Female condoms also protect against STDs but are not as effective as male condoms. Like male condoms, they are available without a prescription.

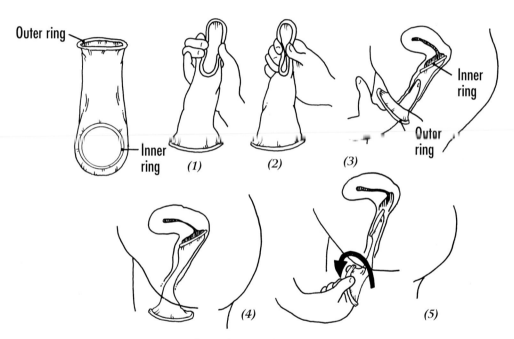

*How to use a female condom: (1) Hold the inner ring of the condom between your thumb and middle finger, (2) squeeze the ring together, (3) insert it into the vagina as far as possible, (4) the outer ring must remain outside the vagina, so hold it in place during intercourse, (5) after intercourse, twist the outer ring to keep the semen inside and stand up while pulling out the condom slowly.*

Their disadvantage is that they are awkward to use and they can slip around during intercourse, allowing semen to escape into the vagina.

## Diaphragm

This is a dome-shaped latex or silicone device with a flexible ring around the edge that is inserted into the vagina before intercourse. It covers the cervix and blocks sperm from entering. The diaphragm must be used with spermicide, a gel formulated to kill sperm. The diaphragm has to stay in place for six hours after

*A diaphragm inside its case*

intercourse, and it is messy to use because of the spermicide. A diaphragm is about as effective at preventing pregnancy as the female condom, but does not protect against STDs. You need a prescription to get one because it has to be fitted to your size by a doctor or other health-care provider.

## Cervical Cap

A cervical cap is a latex or silicone cup that fits over the cervix and is used with spermicide. Like the diaphragm, it prevents sperm from entering the cervix and has to be left in place for at least six hours after intercourse. Its effectiveness is the same as for the diaphragm, and it doesn't protect against STDs. A cervical cap must be fitted, so you need a prescription to get one.

*A cervical cap*

# Hormonal Methods

These methods prevent pregnancy by interrupting the normal process for becoming pregnant, but they don't protect against STDs. For better protection, experts recommend using condoms in addition.

## Birth Control Pills

These pills contain two hormones, and they work by preventing ovulation and by thickening the cervical mucus to prevent sperm from entering. Used properly, they are very effective. A woman must take a pill every day for three weeks, then stop for a week, producing bleeding. These pills are safe and effective,

*Birth control pills in a common case*

they protect against the risk of ovarian and endometrial cancer, and they ease menstrual pain. But there are some disadvantages. You have to remember to take the Pill every day. If you skip days, you might become pregnant. Some women experience nausea, weight gain, spotting, or other side effects. Women who are smokers or who have high blood pressure should not use birth control pills because they have a significant risk of blood clots. Those who want to get pregnant can be successful within one to three months of stopping the Pill.

## Birth Control Injections

A hormone shot (sold as Depo-Provera) is injected by a doctor every three months. The hormone suppresses ovulation and is very effective. It is a popular choice of contraception among young women, but in a study of girls and young women fifteen to nineteen years old published in *The Archives of Pediatrics & Adolescent Medicine*, it was shown to cause bone thinning. The bone loss was reversed when the drug was stopped; after twelve months, no difference was found between women who had never taken Depo-Provera and those who had. However, researchers are still concerned about the possible risks to the bones of girls using this hormone during the time while they are still growing. Using Depo-Provera may also increase the risk of getting the sexually transmitted diseases gonorrhea and chlamydia. The injections are long-lasting, and it might take as long as a year to regain fertility after discontinuing.

## Hormonal Implants

These are tiny matchstick-sized capsules (known as Norplant) placed under the skin of a woman's upper arm. They release a small amount of hormone that prevents pregnancy for a period of up to five years. These are safe and convenient, and a woman can become pregnant as soon as the implants are removed. Inserting the implants and taking them out requires an incision in the skin, which might produce a minimal amount of scarring.

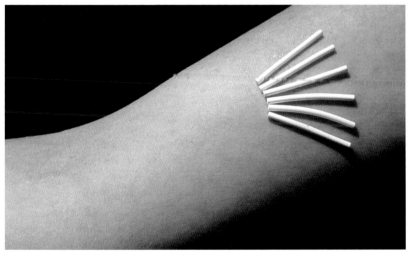

*Six hormonal implants positioned on a woman's arm in the pattern in which they are placed under the skin*

## Vaginal Ring

This is a ring that a woman puts in her vagina and leaves there for three weeks. It releases hormones that prevent pregnancy during that time. She removes it for a week, at which time bleeding occurs. It works the

*A woman holding a vaginal ring*

same way as birth control pills by preventing ovulation and changing the cervical mucus, but the hormones are absorbed through the lining of the vagina instead of in the digestive tract. It is very effective, but if the ring slips out or is removed and is out for more than three hours, additional means of contraception must be used for seven days after reinserting it, in order for the hormones to rise to protective levels again.

## Transdermal Patch

This system (known as Ortho Evra) is a very effective method that involves wearing a patch containing birth control hormones that are absorbed through the skin. It is a small, thin patch that is placed on the arm,

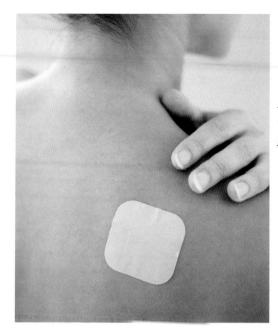

*A woman wearing a transdermal patch*

buttocks, or abdomen once a week for three weeks. For the fourth week, it is left off and bleeding occurs. Like the vaginal ring, the patch releases hormones that work the same way as birth control pills. It doesn't work as well for women who weigh more than 200 pounds (91 kilograms).

## Other Methods
### Intrauterine Device (IUD)
This is a small T-shaped device that is inserted into a woman's uterus by a doctor. One kind contains copper and can remain in place for as long as ten years. Another kind contains a five-year supply of a hormone that prevents pregnancy. They are very effective for preventing pregnancy, and they are

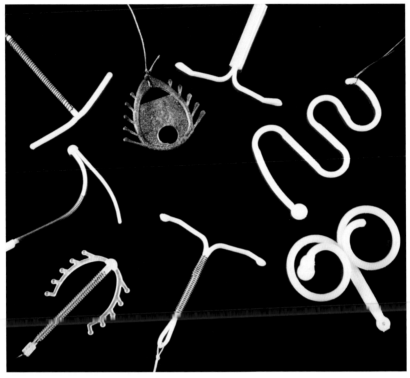

*A variety of intrauterine devices (IUDs)*

convenient because the user doesn't have to do anything before having sex. But IUDs do not protect against STDs, and IUDs can have some unwanted side effects such as spotting between periods, increased menstrual bleeding, cramping, or infection. This method is not recommended for teens because of the side effects.

## Sterilization

This method of contraception is permanent. For a woman, it involves surgery to cut or tie off the fallopian tubes—called tubal ligation—so that sperm and eggs can't meet. Male sterilization—vasectomy—involves cutting and tying the tubes that carry sperm, so when the man ejaculates, his seminal fluid doesn't contain any sperm. Surgical sterilization is only for people who are sure that they do not want children in the future, because operations to reverse these procedures have a low rate of success. Clearly, it's not a suitable method for teens, and doctors will not perform it on them.

## Spermicides

These are sperm-killing jellies, foams, or inserts that are placed in the vagina before intercourse. They don't protect against STDs, and the most commonly used spermicide, nonoxynol-9, may increase the risk of HIV or other STDs because it can irritate the vagina and penis. You can buy spermicides without a prescription, but they are not as reliable as condoms, and they have a high rate of failure if they are not used properly.

## Rhythm Method (natural family planning)

This method involves not having intercourse during the five or six days during the menstrual cycle when a woman is most fertile; in other words, around the time that ovulation occurs, which is about fourteen days before her next period. It is the only method accepted by some religions, and it doesn't involve any devices.

But it's not easy to determine the fertile period; the woman has to keep careful track of her menstrual cycle by examining the cervical mucus and/or taking her body temperature regularly in order to detect the changes that signal ovulation. The failure rate can be high because it's hard to take these measurements every day, many women have an irregular cycle, and sperm can live for several days inside a woman's body.

**Withdrawal**

Removing the penis from the vagina before ejaculation is not a good way to prevent pregnancy because some semen leaks out before ejaculation and because it's difficult to pull out just before ejaculation.

Although these methods are better than nothing, spermicides, the rhythm method, and withdrawal are not very reliable means of contraception.

# Methods That Don't Work

Intercourse during your period isn't safe because some women bleed during ovulation, which is the time you are most fertile. And as noted above, it's hard to determine when ovulation occurs.

Even if you have never had a period, you can get pregnant if you have sex, because the menstrual cycle begins before you start your periods. In other words, you can ovulate and get pregnant before your first period.

Some teens think that urinating after sex will wash the sperm out, but women don't urinate out of the vagina. The opening of the urinary tract is separate and just above the vagina. This is not a way to prevent pregnancy.

Douching is another method that doesn't work. It may even help the sperm swim up toward the egg.

# How to Choose Contraception

If you've chosen to have sex, it's a good idea to consult your health-care provider for advice about which kind of birth control is best for you. You need to remember that even if you use a reliable method such as the Pill, the condom is the only method that provides some protection against STDs. When used properly, condoms are 97 percent safe. Using a condom and the Pill gives you added protection. But no method comes with a guaranteed 100 percent success rate.

# Emergency Contraception

What if you had sex last night and the condom broke? Or maybe you weren't meaning to have intercourse and used no protection at all. Would you know what to do? A medically prescribed emergency contraceptive pill, known as the morning-after pill, can cut your chances of getting pregnant by up to 89 percent if you act quickly. The sooner you start taking the pills, the better your chance of protection. The pills work by delaying ovulation, preventing fertilization, or preventing a fertilized egg from being implanted in the wall of the uterus. According to medical experts, pregnancy does not begin until a fertilized egg is implanted in the lining of a woman's uterus. Emergency contraceptive pills don't work if you are already pregnant.

Emergency contraceptive pills are available only by prescription, making it difficult to obtain them quickly. Some pharmacists refuse to fill the prescriptions for moral reasons. Despite the recommendations of two FDA advisory committees and other

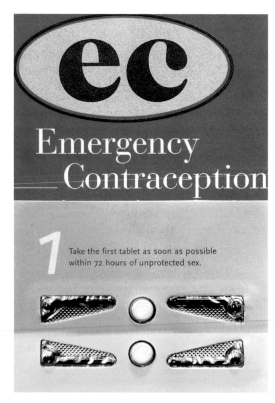

*Many health-care professionals think that if women have easier access to emergency contraception, the number of abortions might be reduced.*

medical authorities, the FDA refused to approve over-the-counter sales of the pills.

## Abortion

Abortion is the voluntary termination of pregnancy. Some women make the decision to have an abortion in order to end an unwanted pregnancy. The issue of abortion is a very controversial and emotionally charged subject, but both abortion opponents and pro-choice advocates agree that abortion is definitely not a good means of birth control.

# Guide to Contraceptives

| Type of Contraceptive | Description | Success Rate | Protection from STDs | Advantages | Disadvantages |
|---|---|---|---|---|---|
| Male condom | Sheath placed over erect penis | Moderate | Best except for abstinence | Non-prescription | Can break or slip |
| Female condom | Sheath covering vagina and cervix | Moderate | Some protection | Non-prescription | Awkward to use; can slip |
| Diaphragm | Dome-shaped rubber disk covering cervix | Moderate | None | Inserted before foreplay or intercourse | Prescription; needs to be fitted |
| Cervical cap | Cup that fits over cervix | Moderate | None | Inserted before foreplay or intercourse | Prescription; difficult to insert |

# Guide to Contraceptives

| Type of Contraceptive | Description | Success Rate | Protection from STDs | Advantages | Disadvantages |
|---|---|---|---|---|---|
| Birth-control pills | Daily hormone pills; prevents ovulation | High | None | Eases menstrual symptoms; may reduce risk of ovarian and endometrial cancer | Prescription; spotting; increased risk of blood clots; must take on schedule |
| Depo-Provera | Hormone injection every three months | Very high | None | Same as for pill | Bone-thinning risk; increased risk of STDs |
| Hormonal implants | Tiny rods surgically implanted under the skin | Very high | None | Prevents pregnancy for up to five years | Requires cutting the skin; expensive |

| Type of Contraceptive | Description | Success Rate | Protection from STDs | Advantages | Disadvantages |
|---|---|---|---|---|---|
| Vaginal ring | Ring inserted in vagina; releases hormones | High | None | Remains in place for 3 weeks, then out for one week | Prescription; other means of contraception must be used if out for more than 3 hours |
| Transdermal patch | Skin patch containing hormones | High | None | Similar to hormone pills | Prescription; less effective in overweight women |
| IUD | Small device inserted in uterus by doctor | High | None | Can remain in place for up to 10 years | Increased bleeding; cramps |
| Sterilization | Surgery to tie off fallopian tubes or vas deferens | Very high | None | Onetime procedure | Reversal usually has low rate of success |

# Guide to Contraceptives

| Type of Contraceptive | Description | Success Rate | Protection from STDs | Advantages | Disadvantages |
|---|---|---|---|---|---|
| Spermicides | Sperm-killing gel, foam, or inserts | Low | None | Non-prescription | Irritation; not reliable |
| Rhythm | Refraining from intercourse during fertile period | Low | None | No devices or pills | Frequent monitoring of body temperature |
| Withdrawal | Removing the penis from the vagina before ejaculation | Low | None | No devices or pills | Semen may leak out before withdrawal |
| Emergency contraceptive pills | Stop or delay ovulation or prevent fertilization or implantation | Moderate | None | Can prevent pregnancy after unprotected intercourse | Prescription; must act quickly |

# Chapter 8

# Working to Prevent Teen Pregnancy and Sexually Transmitted Diseases

Seventeen-year-olds Olivia, Emma, and Ava had placed their orders for vegetable pizzas and Diet Cokes at the pizza parlor where they sat at a small table talking about Emma's younger sister, Grace. Grace had asked Emma if oral sex was safe, and Emma was upset because Grace was only fourteen, too young for sex.

All three of the girls at the pizza place were good friends and had talked to each other about their own sex lives. Today, each of them thought back to the first time they had sex. Olivia was fifteen and in love with a boy five years older. He left her two months after they had sex. Emma and Ava were sixteen and had long-term relationships with boys their age. Now both of them were involved with different boys. All three of the girls said they wished they had waited until they were older before they started having sex. Emma said her sister Grace did not think oral sex was real sex, but the older girls disagreed with her.

Grace had promised to wait for sex until she was married, but her boyfriend was pressuring her for oral sex. Grace told her sister that many of her friends were having oral sex, and they were still virgins, so they were keeping their promises. Emma and her friends were upset with the way the younger kids were starting their sex lives. Before they had finished their pizzas they decided to check on the Web to see what they could do to help kids wait for sex until they were older and could make better choices.

Online, they found the National Day to Prevent Teen Pregnancy (mentioned earlier). Users can find out how they score in a number of situations. For example, here are two typical scenarios:

## Scenario

*12:25 a.m.—Prom after-party*
Kevin knew he made the right choice in bringing Alicia to the prom. He had a feeling she was into him, and tonight she's really showing it. She hasn't taken her eyes off him all night, and now she's led him into an empty room at the after-party.

One problem: Kevin is a lot more nervous than he thought he would be. He's a junior, and he's a virgin. So are most of his friends. He figured "it" would happen tonight. He thought he was ready. All of a sudden, he's not. But she is. What is your advice to Kevin?

a) Keep going! It has to happen some time, so why not now? Who knows when there will be another chance? Relax and go with it.

b) Keep quiet, but if she seems at all unsure, stop. Make her think that you're looking out for her by telling her it's better to wait. Take her back to hang out with your friends.

c) Alicia really likes you and will understand when you tell her you want to take it slow and that you're not ready.

d) Stop and tell her that you really want to do this, but you're afraid someone might come into the room. Tell her you want to wait until you can really be alone.

FACT: Two out of three teens who have sex by age eighteen say they wish they'd waited longer.

The best answer is c, followed by b and d, then a.

## Scenario

*Monday, 5:45 p.m.—After soccer practice*
Erica, Ana, Tanya, and Kim are getting changed after soccer. It is their second season on the team together, and they're getting to be good friends.

TANYA: Kim, you have been SO quiet all day! How'd it go with David this weekend?

KIM: Pretty well. . . . We had fun—a lot of fun, if you guys know what I mean.

ERICA: You mean . . . you did it?

KIM: Well, it's not like we planned on it. It just sort of happened. It wasn't at all what I expected, either.

ERICA: What do you mean? Better? Worse? Tell us everything!

KIM: It was pretty awkward I guess. Isn't that what it was like for you guys?

TANYA: Actually, to be honest, I wouldn't know.

Erica and Ana admit that they wouldn't know either.

KIM: What? You guys haven't done it? Then why did you all say you had?

Ana hasn't said much yet. If you were she, what would you say to Kim?

a) Forget about us; this is about you. You've done it, so we need to know everything. What was it like afterward? Have you talked to him since?

b) I'm so sorry. Sometimes people say they have when they haven't. I wish you had told us you were thinking about doing it so we could have talked about stuff like protection or if you were really ready.

c) Are you ok? How do you feel? Did you use a condom?

d) I'm sorry that this happened, and nothing can change that, but remember that just because you did it once, doesn't mean you have to do it again.

FACT: About 80 percent of teens age twelve to nineteen say they feel pressure to have sex. Everyone is not doing it. In fact, about half of high school-age teens are having sex and half aren't. Sixty-five percent of teens say it would be much easier to delay sex if other teens spoke positively about not having sex.

The best answers are b and d, followed by c, then a.

*(Scenarios are used with permission from the National Campaign to Prevent Teen Pregnancy.)*

More than a half-million teens participate in the National Teen Day quizzes each year. By sharing the National Quiz with groups in your school or other organizations to which you belong, you may help to prevent teen pregnancy.

Many teens work in programs that may help to prevent the spread of AIDS and other STDs. AIDS has been the subject of some teen theater groups, talk shows, radio programs, and numerous articles written by teens.

Shelby Knox from Lubbock, Texas, is a teen who works to change her school's sex education programs. She believes abstinence-only pledges are dangerous because kids who break the pledges are not educated about how to prevent pregnancy and STDs. Since her state has some of the highest rates of teen pregnancy and sexually transmitted diseases in the nation, she decided the students should receive more than the abstinence-only education. Her activism was the subject of a documentary—a Point of View (POV) film on national television (PBS). It was titled *The Education of Shelby Knox* and was first shown in 2005. Although most attempts to change sex education do not become this far-reaching, many young people who participate in their own schools effect change.

Many organizations are glad to include teens in their prevention programs. For example, The Network for Family Life Education at Rutgers University, the State University of New Jersey, has a very successful newsletter, *SEX, ETC.,* that is written by and for teens. Since it began in 1994, it has reached more than 1.5 million teens across the country. You can find current information about it and other newsletters on the Web. See pages 117–118.

*There are many organizations that help educate young people about preventing teen pregnancy and STDs. Here, Aja Cayatano of the Center of Young Women's Development in San Francisco is passing out condoms and counseling teens about safe sex.*

Many other organizations help teens play a part in educating others about delaying sex and preventing teen pregnancy and STDs. Here are some that can help you take action:

- Advocates for Youth, My Voice Counts
  Youth Action Center
  http://www.advocatesforyouth.otrg/youth
  /advocacy/myvoicecounts/sexeducation/qa.htm

- American Red Cross Peer Education
  Training Programs
  Contact the local Red Cross listed in your phone book, or find it on the Web at
  http://www.redcross.org.

- MTV: Music Television and the Kaiser
  Family Foundation
  http://www.mtv.com/onair/ffyr/protect/takeaction
  .jhtml
  There are many suggestions on this page, including petitions to sign, e-mails you can send, and how to become a peer educator.

- National Campaign to Prevent Teen Pregnancy
  http://www.teenpregnancy.org

- Planned Parenthood
  http://www.plannedparenthood.org
  See the "Students Speak Out" section.

- *SEX, ETC.* The Roadmap: A Teen Guide to Changing Your School's Sex Ed
  http://www.sexetc.org/index.php?topic=Roadmap

- SIECUS (Sexuality Information and Education Council of the United States) http://www.siecus.org

- Spiritual Youth for Reproductive Freedom http://www.syrf.org/

There is still much controversy about the teaching of contraception. Most parents want their children to know how to protect themselves from pregnancy and STDs, and most teens want that information. According to a recent poll by the National Campaign to Prevent Teen Pregnancy, 97 percent of young teens want a strong message about not having sex until they are out of high school, and 81 percent said they wish they were getting more information about abstinence and contraception. However, there is a strong movement to discourage the teaching of contraception, and there is a large amount of federal funding that supports abstinence-only education. Although there is agreement on the benefits of waiting for sex until marriage, many teens don't wait. You can take responsibility for whether you wish to enter into a sexual relationship if you know what you will do when it's time to make a decision.

You know that the only foolproof way to avoid pregnancy is not to have sex. You are in control, so you can always say no, even if you have said yes before. How you handle situations depends partly on how much knowledge you have about preventing pregnancy and sexually transmitted diseases, and how you choose to use that knowledge. Everyone has the ability to make his or her own choices and stick with them.

# Glossary

**abstinence:** not having oral, anal, or vaginal sex

**AIDS (acquired immunodeficiency syndrome):** disease resulting from damage to the immune system, caused by infection with HIV. Infections, cancers, and a variety of other conditions develop when the immune system can no longer function properly. Drugs are available to prolong life, but there is no cure.

**anal sex:** when a penis is inserted into an anus

**anus:** the small opening at the end of the digestive tract through which solid waste is expelled

**barrier:** something that blocks things from going through it. Condoms prevent sperm and other body fluids from entering the birth canal. Sheets of latex can prevent diseases from entering another person's body during oral sex.

**birth control:** another term for contraception

**birth-control pills:** hormones in pill form taken by mouth to prevent pregnancy. In the body, the hormones prevent the ovaries from releasing eggs. These pills do not protect against sexually transmitted infections.

**carrier:** A person who is infected with a disease that can be transmitted to another person. Sexually transmitted diseases do not always cause symptoms that can be seen by another person. For example, someone infected with HIV may look healthy.

**cervical cap:** a small rubber cap that fits inside the vagina and is placed over the cervix before intercourse. It is similar to a diaphragm, but smaller.

**cervical secretions:** fluids that come from a woman's cervix through the vagina. Sexually transmitted diseases may be spread to another person by cervical secretions.

**cervix:** the part of a woman's body between the uterus and the vagina. Menstrual blood exits through the opening of the cervix into the vagina. Sperm travel through this part on their way to fertilize an egg.

**clitoris:** small female sex organ located inside the labia. Contains spongy tissue that fills with blood during sexual excitement and is very sensitive to the touch.

**conception:** the moment when a man's sperm fertilizes a woman's egg. This produces a zygote that can grow into an embryo and then become a fetus.

**condom:** a thin cover for a male's penis during intercourse to prevent pregnancy and help prevent STDs

**contraception:** methods people use to prevent pregnancy

**dental dam:** a small piece of latex about 5 inches (13 centimeters) square that should be used when having oral sex with women to help prevent the spread of STDs.

**Depo-Provera®:** a combination of hormones that is injected every three months to protect against pregnancy

**diaphragm:** a small latex cup that fits over a woman's cervix to prevent sperm from reaching an egg

**douching:** washing out the vagina; does not work to prevent pregnancy

**egg:** During the menstrual cycle, an egg is released from an ovary each month and travels by way of a fallopian tube toward the uterus. While in the fallopian tube, the egg can unite with a sperm (become fertilized).

**ejaculation:** the release of semen, which carries sperm through the penis at the time of an orgasm. This release can also take place during a wet dream or masturbation.

**embryo:** when a fertilized egg reaches a certain size, it attaches itself to the inside of the uterus and at the end of two months becomes a fetus

**emergency contraception:** method of preventing pregnancy after unprotected sexual intercourse

**erection:** stiffening and hardening of the penis

**estrogen:** a female hormone produced by the ovaries

**fallopian tubes:** the tubes that connect the ovary to the uterus. There are a pair of tubes, one from each ovary.

**fetus:** an eight-week-old embryo that grows to become a baby

**follicle-stimulating hormone (FSH):** hormone produced by the pituitary gland; stimulates production of sperm and testosterone in boys and maturation of eggs and production of estrogen and progesterone in girls

**genitals:** sex organs; also called private parts

**genital warts:** an STD that appears on a person's genitals

**glans:** another word for the tip of a man's penis

**gonadotrophin-releasing hormone (GnRH):** hormone produced at puberty that acts on the pituitary gland

**gonorrhea:** an STD caused by bacteria

**hepatitis B**: infection caused by a virus that damages the liver. It is spread through infected blood, for example, from contaminated needles shared by drug users, or by sexual intercourse.

**HIV (human immunodeficiency virus):** a virus that destroys the immune system and causes AIDS. *See* AIDS.

**hormones:** chemical messengers that control many body functions

**human papilloma virus (HPV):** an STD that causes genital warts. It can cause cancer of the cervix in women.

**hymen:** a thin piece of skin with a small opening that stretches over the vagina. An intact hymen is found in virgins, but girls who break or stretch this thin skin in sports or by using tampons are still considered virgins.

**immune system:** complicated system of cells and chemical secretions that protect the body from germs and other invaders. HIV gradually destroys this system.

**implants:** a kind of birth control in which hormones are released from small, soft tubes that are placed in a woman's body to prevent pregnancy

**intrauterine device (IUD):** a T-shaped device that contains either a hormone or copper that is inserted into the uterus to prevent pregnancy

**labia:** two folds of skin that form the lips of the vagina

**love:** three stages are lust, infatuation, and attachment. Lust is immediate sexual attraction, or "love at first sight." Infatuation is often called being in love and is a stage that lasts from a year and a half to three years in which lovers idealize each other. Attachment is a long-term relationship with feelings of security and contentment.

**lubricant:** a substance that makes something slippery. Water-based lubricants are often used on the outer surface of condoms.

**luteinizing hormone (LH):** hormone produced by the pituitary. Like FSH, it acts on the sex organs of males and females.

**menstruation:** monthly bleeding in females as part of a cycle that includes ovulation. Does not occur during pregnancy.

**Mullerian ducts:** embryonic structures that develop into female sex organs

**orgasm:** sudden release of muscular tension and blood that accumulates in the genital area, accompanied by intense pleasure

**ovary:** one of the paired female sex organs. Contains eggs and produces female hormones.

**ovulation:** the release of an egg from the ovary

**penis:** male sex organ

**premarital sex:** sex before marriage

**reproductive organs:** male and female sex organs

**rhythm method:** a method of birth control that depends on determining the days when a woman is fertile. Not a reliable method of birth control.

**scrotum:** sac of wrinkly skin containing the testes in males

**semen:** the whitish sperm bearing fluid that is ejaculated during the male orgasm. It consists of secretions from the prostate gland, seminal vesicles, and Cowper's glands.

**sexuality:** expressing one's sex, male or female

**sperm:** male sex cell

**spermicide:** jelly, foam, or insert containing substances that kill sperm; not as effective as condoms

**sterilization:** surgery to tie off fallopian tubes or vas deferens; permanent, very effective means of birth control

**syphilis:** infection transmitted by sexual contact. If left untreated, it spreads throughout the body, causing severe damage to the brain, nerves, heart and blood vessels, digestive system, and other organs.

**testis (plural: testes):** also called testicles. Contain tubules where sperm are made and the male hormone testosterone is produced.

**testosterone:** male hormone

**transdermal patch:** patch containing birth-control hormones, worn on the skin

**trichomoniasis:** a sexually transmitted disease that is caused by a parasite

**urethra:** tube that carries urine from the bladder to the outside of the body. In males, it also carries semen.

**uterus:** pear-shaped organ in which the embryo develops during pregnancy

**vagina:** birth canal. Extends from the uterus to the vulva.

**vas deferens:** tube that carries semen

**venereal disease:** another term for diseases now usually called sexually transmitted infections (STIs) or sexually transmitted diseases (STDs)

**vulva:** external genitals of a female

**Wolffian ducts:** embryonic structures that develop into male sex organs

# For Further Information

## Books

Bell, Ruth. *Changing Bodies, Changing Lives: A Book for Teens on Sex and Relationships*, Third Edition. New York: Crown Publishing Group, 1998.

Brynie, Faith Hickman. *101 Questions about Reproduction or How One + One = Three or Four or More*. Minneapolis, MN: Twenty-First Century Books, 2006.

Brynie, Faith Hickman. *101 Questions about Sex and Sexuality with Answers for the Curious, Cautious, and Confused*. Minneapolis, MN: Twenty-First Century Books, 2003.

Hatchel, Deborah. *What Smart Teenagers Know About Dating, Relationships and Sex*. Santa Barbara, CA: Piper Press, 2001.

Hyde, Margaret O., and Elizabeth Forsyth. *AIDS: What Does It Mean to You?* New York: Walker and Company, 1996.

Lichona, Tom and Judy. *Sex, Love and You: Making the Right Decision.* Notre Dame, IN: Ava Maria Press, 2003.

Madaras, Lynda. *What's Happening to My Body? Book for Boys: A Growing Up Guide for Parents and Sons*, Third Edition. New York: Newmarket Press, 2000.

Madaras, Lynda. *What's Happening to My Body? Book for Girls: A Growing Up Guide for Parents and Daughters*, Third Edition. New York: Newmarket Press, 2000.

McWilliams, Kelly. *Doormat.* New York: Delacorte Press, 2004. (Fiction)

Moe, Barbara. *Everything You Need to Know About Abstinence.* New York: Rosen Press, 1998.

# Hotlines & Organizations

American Red Cross
National Teenage AIDS Hotline: 1-800-440-TEEN
Hours: Friday and Saturday, 6 P.M. till Midnight EST
> Staff of peer educators provides information about HIV/AIDS and other STDs

American Social Health Association
National Herpes Hotline: 1-919-361-8488
> Provides herpes information, counseling, and referrals to local support groups

Association of Reproductive Health Professionals
Emergency Contraception Hotline
1-888-NOT2LATE
> Prerecorded information about emergency contraception and names and phone numbers of places where you can get emergency contraception

Black Entertainment Television/Kaiser Family Foundation
1-866-RAP-IT-UP
> Provides information on safe sex and reproductive health

Centers for Disease Control and Prevention (CDC)
National HIV and AIDS Hotline: 1-800 342 AIDS
National STD and AIDS Hotline: 1-800-227-8922
Spanish: 1-800-344-7432
TYY/Deaf access: 1-800-243-7889
 Answers questions about symptoms, testing, and prevention; provides referrals

Gay and Lesbian National Hotline
1-888-843-4564
 Provides free and anonymous information, referrals, and peer counseling

Kaiser Family Foundation and MTV-Kaiser Family
Foundation
It's Your (Sex) Life
1-888-BE-SAFE
 Booklet and connections to other safe sex hotlines

National HPV Hotline
1-877-HPV-5868
 Answers questions about human papillomavirus

# Websites

Adolescent Wellness and Reproductive Education
Foundation:
http://www.awarefoundation.org

Advocates for Youth:
http://www.advocatesforyouth.org/teens

The Alan Guttmacher Institute:
http://www.alanguttmacher.org and http://www.agi-usa.org

American Social Health Association:
http://www.iwannaknow.org and http://www.ashastd.org

The Association of Reproductive Health Professionals:
http://www.arhp.org/choosing

Centers for Disease Control:
http://www.cdc.gov/nchstp/dstd/dstdp.html

Kaiser Family Foundation/MTV:
http://www.fightforyourrights.mtv.com

Kaiser Family Foundation/MTV (Sexual Health for African Americans):
http://www.bet.com/health/sexualhealth

Kaiser Family Foundation/Viacom:
http://www.knowhivaids.org

National Campaign to Prevent Teen Pregnancy:
http://www.teenpregnancy.org

National Institutes of Health:
http://www.nlm.nih.gov/medlineplus/birthcontrol
.html#teenagers

Nemours Foundation:
http://www.kidshealth.org

Planned Parenthood Federation of America:
www.plannedparenthood.org and http://www.teenwire.com

Rutgers, the State University of New Jersey:
http://www.sexetc.org

Sexuality Information and Education Council of the
United States (SIECUS):
http://www.siecus.org

*Teen People:*
http://www.teenpeople.com

University of California:
http://www.whatudo.org

# Source Notes

p. 12  Princeton Survey Research Associates International, NBC/*People*: National Survey of Young Teens' Sexual Attitudes and Behaviors, 2004, p. 17.

p. 12  National Campaign to Prevent Teen Pregnancy, "Science Says: Teens and Oral Sex," Number 17, September 2005, p. 1.

p. 13  "Putting What Works to Work," National Campaign to Prevent Teen Pregnancy, "Science Says: American Opinion on Teen Pregnancy and Related Issues 2003," Number 7, February 2004, p. 2.

p. 14  Jessemyn Pekari, "From the Field: Just Say Yes Helps Get Abstinence Education Into Texas Public Schools," October 10, 2004, Abstinence Clearinghouse E-Mail Update.

p. 14  General Facts and Stats, National Campaign to Prevent Teen Pregnancy, February 2004, p. 1.

p. 16  Bill Albert, "With One Voice 2004: America's Adults and

Teens Sound Off About Teen Pregnancy," Washington, DC: The National Campaign to Prevent Teen Pregnancy, p. 5.

p. 17    Karen Katz and William Finger, "Sexuality and Family Life Education Helps Prepare Young People," YouthLens on Reproductive Health and HIV/AIDS, Number 2, 2002, p. 1.

p. 17    National Campaign to Prevent Teen Pregnancy, General Facts and Stats, p.1, February 2004.

p. 17    "How Do You Score? The Fourth Annual National Day to Prevent Teen Pregnancy will be May 4, 2005." <http://www.teenpregnancy.org/national/default.asp>

p. 18    "Teens Delaying Sexual Activity, Using Contraception More Effectively," National Center for Health Statistics, Fact Sheet for Series 23, November 24, 2004. <http:/www.cdc.gov/factstats/reprodu.htm>

p. 20    General Facts and Stats, National Campaign to Prevent Teen Pregnancy, Research Resources and Information, February 2004, p. 1.

p. 20    Amanda Gardner, "Sexual Content on TV Spurs Teens Into Action," 2004, <http://www.healthday.com/view.cfm?ld=521064>

p. 22    "SIECUS Applauds the Introduction of the Responsible Education about Life Act, 2005, <http://www.siecus.oerg/media/press00 90.html>

p. 22    "More U.S. Teens Say They're Putting Sex On Hold," *Christian Science Monitor,* December 13, 2004.

p. 24    American Opinion on Teen Pregnancy and Related Issues 2003, National Campaign to Prevent Teen Pregnancy, *Science Says,* Number 7, February 2003, p. 3.

p. 27    "Washington State HIV/AIDS Council Asks Governor to Reject Abstinence-Only-Until-Marriage Title V Funding," SIECUS Policy Update, January 2003, accessed 16 February 2004.

p. 28    Princeton Survey Research Associates International, "NBC/People National Survey of Young Teens Sexual Attitudes and Behaviors," Topline Report, p. 13, Broadcast NBC, January 26, 2005.

p. 28    Abstinence Clearinghouse, Latest News: Teen Virginity Pledges Lead to Better Life Outcomes, Study Finds, <http://abstinence.net/library/index/php?entryid=1396>

p. 28    Douglas Kirby, Emerging Answers: Research Findings on Programs to Reduce Teen Pregnancy, The National

Campaign to Reduce Teen Pregnancy, 2001.

p. 28 Why Rates are Declining: New Research Cites Less Sex and More Contraception, Washington, DC: The National Campaign to Prevent Teen Pregnancy, Campaign Update, Fall 2004, p. 5.

p. 29 <http://www.naral.org/about/newsroom/presrealse /pr120204_abstinence.cfm?renderforpri>

p. 29 Study Finds Many Errors in Ohio Abstinence-Only Programs, <http://www.teenwire.com/flash/fl_mainpage.asp>

p. 29 "Adolescents Who Take Virginity Pledges Have Lower rates of Out-of-Wedlock Births," <http://.www.geiertage.org/Research/Family/cda04-04.cfm>

p. 29 Peggy Peck, "AMA Cool to Some Abstinence-Only Sex Ed," <http://my.webmd.com/content/article/98 /104651?printing=true>

p. 29 Priscilla Pardini, "Abstinence-Only Education Continues to Flourish," Rethinking Schools Online, <http://www.rethinkingschools.org/sex/Abst172.shtm>

p. 30 Steven D. Schafersman, "Health Education Textbook Review and Analysis," Texas Citizens for Science, 2004, p 2.

p. 30 Alan Singer, "Preaching Ain't Teaching: Sex Education and America's New Puritans." Rethinking Schools Online, <http://www.rethinkingschools.org/wex/preach/shtml>

p. 31 "ACLU Asks Louisiana to Remove Religious Content from Abstinence-Only Website, Citing Numerous Violations of 2002 Agreement," media@aclu.org, November 17, 2004.

p. 31 "ACLU Troubled by Court's Refusal to Hold Louisiana Governor's Program on Abstinence in Contempt for Continuing to Preach with Taxpayer Dollars," <http://www.aclu.org/ReproductiveRights/Reproductive Rights.cfm?ID=18577&c=30>, June 24, 2005.

p. 31 "ACLU Tells Feds to Abstain from Christian Education Program," <http://www.mtv.com/news/articles/1502494 /05172005/id_0.jhtml?headline>

p. 31 "In Light of ACLU Lawsuit Charging the Federal Government with Funding Religious Activities, The Silver Ring Thing Removes Religious Content from Website," <http://www.aclu.org/news/NewsPrint.cfm?ID=18280&c=3 0>, May 19, 2005.

p. 31 Joycelyn Elders, "Vows of Abstinence Break More Easily Than Latex Condoms," Rethinking Schools Online,

&lt;http://www.rethinkingschools.org/sex/elders.shtml&gt;

p. 32   Nicholas D. Kristof, "When Marriage Kills," *The New York Times,* March 30, 2005.

p. 33   Joseph Loconte, The ABCs of AIDS, &lt;http://www.heritage.org/Press/Commentary/ev102203a .cfm?RenderforPrint=1&gt;

p. 34   "Love is Better Than Condoms in War Against AIDS, Says Museveni," &lt;http://www.highbeam.com/library/doc3 .asp?ctrlInfo=Round9c%3AProd%3ADOC%3Aprin&gt;

p. 34   United States Agency for International Development, Annual Program Statement: HIV/AIDS through Abstinence and Healthy Choices for Youth: President's Emergency Plan for AIDS Relief. [APS No.M/OP-04-812] Washington, DC: USAID, March 11, 2004, p. 8.

p. 36   &lt;http://www.siecus.org/policy/states/2004/analysis.html&gt;

p. 40   National Campaign to Prevent Teen Pregnancy, "Teen Pregnancy—So What?" 2004, &lt;http://www.teenpregnancy.org/whycare/sowhat.asp&gt;

p. 41   Teen Sex and Pregnancy, "Facts in Brief," Allan Guttmacher Institute, 1999

p. 41   Ibid.

p. 41   Ibid.

p. 41   YouthLens on Reproductive Health and HIV/AIDS, "Maternal Health Care Among Adolescents," Number 11, 2004, p. 1.

p. 41   National Campaign to Prevent Teen Pregnancy, "Teen Pregnancy–So What?" 2004, &lt;http://www.teenpregnancy.org/whycare/sowhat.asp&gt;

p. 42   Weimann, Constance and others, "Are Pregnant Adolescents Stigmatized by Pregnancy?" Journal of Adolescent Health, Vol. 36, Issue 4, April 2005, p. 352.

p. 44   Weinstock, H., S. Berman, W. Cates, "Sexually Transmitted Diseases Among American Youth: Incidence and Prevalence Estimates, 2000," *Perspectives on Sexual and Reproductive Health* 2004; 36 (1):6-10.

p. 44   Bruckner, Hannah, and Peter Bearman, "After the Promise: The STD Consequences of Adolescent Virginity Pledges," *Journal of Adolescent Health,* Volume 36, Issue 4, April 2005, pages 271-278.

p. 45   Lawrence K. Altman, "Studies Rebut Earlier Report on Pledges of Virginity," *The New York Times,* June 15, 2005.

p. 45   Claudia Wallis, "A Snapshot of Teen Sex," *Time,* February 7, 2005, p. 58.

p. 47   CDC STD Prevention, "Most Teens Not Provided with STD or Pregnancy Prevention Counseling during Checkups." <http:www.cdc.org/nchstp.dstd/Press_Release/Teens2000 .htm>

p. 47   "The New Face of AIDS," *The Economist,* November 27, 2004, p. 83.

p. 49   "Thailand Achieves Sustained Reduction in HIV Infection Rates," <http://www.who.int/inf-new/aids1.htm>

p. 60   Lawrence K. Altman, "More Living with H.I.V., But Concerns Remain," *The New York Times,* June 14, 2005.

p. 62   National Campaign to Prevent Teen Pregnancy, "Science Says: American Opinion on Teen Pregnancy and Related Issues," 2003, Number 7, February 2003, p. 1.

p. 63   Ibid.

p. 64   "Surgeon General Calls for Dialogue on Sexuality," June 28, 2001, <http://dailynews.yahoo.com/h/nm/20010628/hl/sexuality_1.html>

p. 65   Planned Parenthood Federation of America, Abstinence Only "Sex" Education, Fact Sheet, pp. 3-4.

p. 65   Julie Sabatier, "Speaking Out about Sex Ed!" <http://www.teenwire.com/infocus/2003/if_20031125p265_ed.asp>

p. 66   Sheila Gibbons, "A Brief History of Contraceptive Ads," <http://www.plannedparenthood.org/articles/041231-advertisements.html>

p. 66   "More Mention of Abstinence, Consequences of Intercourse, 'Safer Sex' on Television Shows," Kaiser Daily Reproductive Health Report, February 5, 2003.

p. 66   Collins, Rebecca L., and others, "Entertainment Television as a Healthy Sex Educator," *Pediatrics,* Vol. 112, November 2003, p. 1115-1121.

p. 67   "Sex on American Television: An Analysis Across Program Genres and Network Types,"<http://www.highbeam.com/library/doc3.asp?ctrlInfo=Round93c%3APRod%3ADOC%3Apri>

p. 67   Ibid.

p. 67   "Reaching Young Adults Through Entertainment," Population Reports, Series J, Number 41. <http://www.infoforhealth.org/pr/j41/j41reach.shmtl>

p. 68   Collins, Rebecca L., and others, "RAND Study Finds Adolescents Who Watch a Lot of TV With Sexual Content Have Sex Sooner," *Pediatrics,* Vol. 114, September 2004, p. 280-289.

p. 69   Lara Weisstuch, "Sexism in Rap Sparks Black Magazine to Say, 'Enough,' *Christian Science Monitor,* January 12, 2005.

p. 80   U.S. Department of Health and Human Services: Office of Public Health and Science—Office of Population Affairs. "What You Should Know About Contraception!" *Teen Talk* #3, March, 2003.

p. 81   It's Your (Sex) Life: Your Guide to Safe and Responsible Sex, p. 6, Henry J. Kaiser Foundation, Publication Number 1311, Apr. 1, 2002.

p. 81   Kaiser Daily Reproductive Health Report, <http://www.kaisernetwork.org>, downloaded March 10, 2004.

p. 81   It's Your (Sex) Life: Your Guide to Safe and Responsible Sex, p. 16, Henry J. Kaiser Foundation, Publication Number 1311, Apr. 1, 2002.

p. 88   nytimes.com, February 8, 2005, "Patterns: Your Bones on Birth Control".

p. 88   "Depo Provera Appears to Increase Risk for Chlamydial and Gonococcal Infections," *NIH News,* National Institutes of Health, August 24, 2004.

p. 95   NOT-2-LATE.com

p. 108   "ACLU Tells Feds To Abstain From Christian Sex-Ed Program," <http://www.mtv.com/news/articles/1502494/05172005/id_0.jhml?headline>

# Index

Page numbers in *italics* refer to illustrations.

ABC program, 33
Abortion, 16, 59, 96
Abstinence, 17–36
    abstinence-only educa-
      tion, 26–31, 36, 59, 63–65
    as new sexual revolution,
      19, 22–25, *23*
    reasons for, 26–27
    teen comments on, 35–36
    in Uganda, 33–35, *34*
Abstinence Clearinghouse, 14, 29
*Abstinence-Only Curricula Contain*
    *False Information* (Waxman
    report), 28–29
Adoption, 59
Advocates for Youth, My Voice
    Counts Youth Action
    Center, 107
Age of consent, 4
AIDS (acquired immunodeficiency
    syndrome), 10, 15, 18,
    32–35, 45, 49, 57
American Civil Liberties Union
    (ACLU), 31
American Heritage Foundation, 29,
    33
American Medical Association
    (AMA), 29
American Red Cross Peer
    Education Training Pro-
    grams, 107
Anal sex, 28, 45
Antibiotic drugs, 46, 51, 53
Antiviral drugs, 52
Anus, 77

Barrier methods of contraception,
    82–86
Billboards, 70
Birth control (*see* Contraception)
Birth control injections, 88, 98
Birth control pills, *87*, 87–88, 98

Cayatano, Aja, 106, *106*
Centers for Disease Control
    (CDC), 43, 49
Cervical cancer, 53, 82
Cervical cap, 86, 97
Cervix, 77, 78
Chancroid, 51
Chastity rings, 24–25
Chlamydia, 50, 51, 54–55, 88
Circumcision, 74
Clitoris, 77
Condoms, 15, 30
    directions for use, *83, 84*
    effectiveness of, 66, 81–82
    female, *84,* 84–85, 97
    increased use of, 19
    male, *82,* 82–83, 97
    sexually transmitted dis-
      eases (STDs) and, 33–34,
      44, 46, 48–50
Contraception, 80–100 (*see also*
    Abstinence)
    advertising and, 67–68
    barrier methods, 82–86
    birth control injections,
      88, 98
    birth control pills, *87,*
      87–88, 98
    cervical cap, 86, 97

condom (*see* Condoms)
diaphragm, *85,* 85–86, 97
emergency, 95–96, *96,* 100
guide to, 97–100
hormonal implants, 89, *89,* 98
hormonal methods, 87–91
information, 61–65, 108
intrauterine device (IUD), 91–92, *92,* 99
learning about, 16–17
rhythm method, 38, 93–94, 100
spermicides, 85, 93, 94, 100
sterilization, 92–93, 99
talking about, 15
transdermal patch, 90–91, 99
vaginal ring, 89–90, *90,* 99
withdrawal, 58, 62, 94, 100
Couric, Katie, 12, 68
Cowper's glands, 75
Crabs, 31

Dental dams, 83
Depo-Provera, 88, 98
Depression, 13, 46, 55
Diaphragm, *85,* 85–86, 97
Douching, 61, 94

Eggs, 75, 78
Ejaculation (coming), 75, 79
Emergency contraception, 95–96, *96,* 100
Epididymis, 75
Erectile tissue, 78
Erection, 78–79
Estrogen, 72, 75, 77

Fallopian tubes (oviducts), 77, 78, 92
Family planning clinics, 65
Female condoms, *84,* 84–85, 97
Female sex organs, 75, *76,* 77–78
Fertilization, 38, 72–73, 78

Follicle-stimulating hormone (FSH), 72
Foreskin, 74
*Friends* (television show), 66
"Friends with benefits," 11, 46

Gay and lesbian youth, 27
Genital herpes, 45, 52
Genitals (*see* Sex organs)
Genital warts, 53, 82
Glans, 74
Gonadotrophin-releasing hormone (GnRH), 72
Gonorrhea, 45–47, 50, 51, 88

Healy, Sean, 33
Hepatitis B, 52
Herpes, 45, 52
High blood pressure, 41
Hip-hop culture, 69
HIV (human immunodeficiency virus), 18, 49, 52, 60
Homosexuality, 57–58
Hooking up, 10–12, 46
Hormonal implants, 89, *89,* 98
Human papillomavirus (HPV), 53, 82
Hymen, 77

Implants, hormonal, 89, *89,* 98
Incest, 47
Independence, 15
Infertility, 46
Infidelity, 13
Internet, 69–70
Intrauterine device (IUD), 91–92, *92,* 99

Kaiser Family Foundation, 67, 107
Knox, Shelby, 105

Labia, 77
Labor and childbirth, 41
Low birth weight, 41
Lubricants, 83

Luteinizing hormone (LH), 72

Magazines, 70
Male condoms, *82*, 82–83, 97
Male sex organs, 73–75, *74*
Masturbation, 55
Media, sexual scenes in, 20, *21*,
       66–70
Menstruation, 20, 38, 78, 94
Metronidazole, 53
Morning-after pill, 95
MTV: Music Television, 67, 107
Mullerian ducts, 72
Music and music videos, 68–69

National AIDS Hotline, 50
National Campaign to Prevent
       Teen Pregnancy, 16, 69,
       105, 107, 108
National Center for Health
       Statistics, 18
National Coalition against
       Censorship, 30
National Day to Prevent Teen
       Pregnancy, 69, 102, 105
National Education Association
       (NEA), 30
NBC/*People* National Survey of
       Young Teens' Sexual Atti-
       tudes and Behaviors, 12,
       28, 68
Network for Family Life Education,
       106
Nonoxynol-9, 93
Norplant, 89

Obesity, 41
Oral sex, 10–12, 28, 45, 46, 83,
       101, 102
Orgasm, 79
Ortho Evra, 90
Ovaries, 75
Ovulation, 38, 75, 77–78, 93, 94

Parents, as sex educators, 62–63

Penis, 71, 73, 74, 77–79
Period (*see* Menstruation)
Pituitary gland, 72
Planned Parenthood, 65, 107
Posters, 70
Pregnancy, 13, 14, 22
       incidence of teenage, 17,
       20–22, 80–81
       medical problems during,
       41
       teen parenting, 39–43, 59
Progesterone, 72, 77
Prostate gland, 75, 79
Puberty, 71–72, 75
Pubic lice, 51
Pure Love Alliance, 26, *26*

RAND Corporation, 66, 67
Religion, 13, 16, 25, 30–31
Reproductive organs (*see* Sex
       organs)
Rhythm method (natural family
       planning), 38, 93–94, 100

Scrotum, 74
Semen, 75
Seminal vesicles, 75, 79
Sex education, 17, 43, 55
       abstinence-only, 26–31,
       36, 59, 63–65
       family planning clinics, 65
       parents and, 62–63
       in schools, 63–65,
       105–106
*SEX, ETC.* The Roadmap: A Teen
       Guide to Changing Your
       School's Sex Ed, 106, 107
Sex hormones, 72, 75, 77
Sex organs, 72
       female, 75, *76*, 77–78
       male, 73–75, *74*
Sexual abuse, 27, 41
Sexual activity
       abstinence and (*see*
       Abstinence)

anal sex, 28, 45
arousal, 78–79
contraception (*see*
Contraception)
laws and, 14
media's portrayal of, 20,
*21*, 66–70
oral sex, 10–12, 28, 45,
46, 83, 101, 102
positions, 61
readiness for, 5–18
saying no, 7–9
secret lives of teens, 54–60
Sexual fantasies, 55
Sexuality Information and Education Council of the
United States (SIECUS),
43, 108
Sexually transmitted diseases
(STDs), 13
abstinence and, 22
anal sex and, 45
avoiding, 43–47
contraception and, 33–34,
44, 46, 48–50, 81–84,
86–88, 92, 93, 95, 97–100
incidence of, 43, 81
information about
common, 51–53
oral sex and, 10, 12, 28,
45, 46
spreading, 47–50
symptoms of, 50
testing for, 15, 38–39, 44
Sexual revolution, 19–20
Shaft, 74
Silver Ring Thing, 31
Sinding, Steven, 33
Single mothers, 21, 40
Sperm, 72–75, *73*, 78
Spermicides, 85, 93, 94, 100
Spiritual Youth for Reproductive
Freedom, 108
Stacher, David, 64

Sterilization, 92–93, 99
Syphilis, 45, 53

"Take Back the Music" campaign,
69
Teen parenting, 39–43, 59
Testes (testicles), 71, 73–75
Testosterone, 72, 74
Thailand, 49
Transdermal patch, 90–91, 99
Trichomoniasis, 50, 53
True Love Waits, 25
Tubal ligation, 92

Urethra, 75, 77
Uterus, 75, 78

Vagina, 77–79
Vaginal ring, 89–90, *90*, 99
Vas deferens, 75, 79
Vasectomy, 92–93
Venereal disease (*see* Sexually
transmitted diseases
(STDs))
Virginity, 20, 23, 77
Virginity pledges, 24–25, 29, 31, 37,
44, 58, 81

Waxman, Henry, 28
Withdrawal, 58, 62, 94, 100
Wolffian ducts, 72, 77
World AIDS Day (2004), 32–33
World Health Organization
(WHO), 16

Zambia, 32